**Market
Structure and
Performance**

Market Structure and Performance

The U.S. Food Processing Industries

Blake Imel
U.S. Department of Agriculture

Michael R. Behr
University of Wisconsin, Superior

Peter G. Helmberger
University of Wisconsin, Madison

Lexington Books
D.C. Heath and Company
Lexington, Massachusetts
Toronto   London

Copyright © 1972 by D.C. Heath and Company.

All rights reserved. No part of this publication may be reproduced or transmitted in any form or by any means, electronic or mechanical, including photocopy, recording, or any information storage or retrieval system, without permission in writing from the publisher, except for the purposes of the U.S. Government.

Published simultaneously in Canada.

Printed in the United States of America.

International Standard Book Number: 0-669-83899-3.

Library of Congress Catalog Card Number: 72-467.

Table of Contents

List of Tables and Figures	vi
Foreword *by Willard F. Mueller*	xi
Preface	xv
Introduction	1
Chapter 1 The Economic Framework and Some Problems of Application	5
Chapter 2 Estimation Procedures	17
Chapter 3 Sample Selection and Survey Procedure	29
Chapter 4 Industry Definitions	33
Chapter 5 Structure-Profit Relationships	37
Chapter 6 Structure-Progress Relationships	65
Chapter 7 Error Components in Aggregative Analyses	77
Chapter 8 Major Findings	85
Appendix A	89
Appendix B	99
Notes	107
Index	113
About the Authors	117

List of Tables and Figures

Tables

3-1	Sample of Companies	30
3-2	Number of Sample Companies Classified According to Primary Sector	31
5-1	Ninety-nine Food Sector Companies: Estimated Regression Equations Relating Profit over Sales (R_i) to Three Explanatory Variables Using Classical Least Squares (CLS) and Using Generalized Least Squares (GLS) with Three Alternative Specifications of the Variance-Covariance Matrix of the Error Term	48
5-2	Ninety-nine Food Sector Companies: Estimated Regression Equations Relating Profit over Sales (R_i) to Three Explanatory Variables Using Classical Least Squares (CLS) and Using Generalized Least Squares (GLS) with Three Alternative Specifications of Variance-Covariance Matrix of the Error Term, Reconstructed Census Product Categories, National Market Areas	51
5-3	Average Squared Residuals from Equations Estimated in Table 5-1 for the Reconstructed Census Industries by Quartile, Ordering Based on Characteristics of the Firm	52
5-4	Ninety-nine Food Sector Companies: Estimated Regression Equations Relating Total Returns to Total Assets (R'_i) and Profit over Net Worth (R''_i) to Three Explanatory Variables Using Classical Least Squares (CLS) and Using Generalized Least Squares (GLS) with One Specification of the Variance-Covariance Matrix of the Error Term, Reconstructed Census Industries, and Census Four-Digit Industries	54
5-5	Ninety-nine Food Sector Companies: Estimated Regression Equations Relating Profit over Sales (R_i) to Various Explanatory Variables Using Generalized Least Squares (GLS) with Omega Ratio Equal to 0.5, Reconstructed Census Industries	56
5-6	Classical Least Squares Regression Estimates of Rate of Profit on Sales (R_i) for Nine Reconstructed Census Concentration Classifications—Based on Weighted Binary Estimates of Equation 5-9 with Y_{1i} and Y_{2i} Held at Their Mean Sample Values	63
6-1	Ninety-eight Food Sector Companies: Estimated Regression	

	Equations Relating R and D Expenditures Divided by Sales (Y_{2i}) to Five Explanatory Variables Using Classical Least Squares (CLS) and Using Generalized Least Squares (GLS) with Three Alternative Specifications of the Variance-Covariance Matrix of the Error Term	70
6-2	Ninety-eight Food Sector Companies: Estimated Regression Equations Relating Patents Divided by Sales (Y'_{2i}) to Five Explanatory Variables Using Classical Least Squares (CLS) and Using Generalized Least Squares (GLS) with Three Alternative Specifications of the Variance-Covariance Matrix of the Error Term	74
A-1	Reconstructed Census Industries: Four-Firm and Eight-Firm Concentration Percentages, 1963, and Market Growth Rates, 1954–1963	90
A-2	Census Four-Digit Industries: Four-Firm and Eight-Firm Concentration Percentages, 1963; Market Shares of Minimum-Optimum Sized Plants, 1963; and Market Growth Rates, 1958–1963	94
A-3	Census Four-Five-Digit Industries: Four-Firm and Eight-Firm Concentration Percentages, 1963, and Market Growth Rates, 1958–1963	96
B-1	Four-Firm Weighted Concentration Ratios of Ninety-nine Food Processing Companies, Ranked Using Reconstructed Census Industry Definitions with Corresponding Figures for Census Four-Digit and Four-Five-Digit Definitions	99
B-2	Ninety-nine Food Sector Companies: Estimated Regression Equations Relating Total Returns to All Assets (R'_i) to Three Explanatory Variables using Classical Least Squares (CLS) and Using Generalized Least Squares (GLS) with Three Alternative Specifications of the Variance-Covariance Matrix of the Error Term and Using Alternative Industry Definitions	100
B-3	Ninety-nine Food Sector Companies: Estimated Regression Equations Relating Profit over Net Worth (R''_i) to Three Explanatory Variables Using Classical Least Squares (CLS) and Using Generalized Least Squares (GLS) with Three Alternative Specifications of the Variance-Covariance Matrix of the Error Term and Using Alternative Industry Definitions	102
B-4	Ninety-nine Food Sector Companies: Estimated Regression Equations Relating Profit over Sales (R_i) to Four Explanatory Variables Using Classical Least Squares (CLS)	

LIST OF TABLES AND FIGURES ix

	and Using Generalized Least Squares (GLS) with One Specification of the Variance-Covariance Matrix of the Error Term, Concentration Based on Alternative Industry Definitions	104
B-5	Ninety-nine Food Sector Companies: Estimated Regression Equations Relating Profit over Sales (R_i) to Combinations of Five Independent Explanatory Variables Using Classical Least Squares (CLS) and Using Generalized Least Squares (GLS) with Three Alternative Specifications of the Variance-Covariance Matrix of Error Terms, Reconstructed Census Industries	105
B-6	Ninety-nine Food Sector Companies: Estimated Regression Equations Relating Profit over Sales (R_i) to Combinations of Five Independent Explanatory Variables Using Classical Least Squares (CLS) and Using Generalized Least Squares (GLS) with Three Alternative Specifications of the Variance-Covariance Matrix of the Error Term, Census Four-Digit Industries	106

Figures

1-1	Equilibrium Given a Monopolized Industry Producing Product B and a Competitive Industry Producing Product A	9
5-1	Alternative Classical Least Squares Estimates (CLS) of the Relationship Between Rate of Profit on Sales (R_i) and the Four-Firm Concentration Ratio (M_{1j}) for the Reconstructed Census Industries—Net Regressions for Linear (Table 5-1) and Weighted Binary (Equation 5.9) Variables	64

Foreword

When America put into effect the Sherman Act in 1890, it embarked on a unique social experiment. With no significant exceptions, ours is the only nation to have pursued for so long a policy of maintaining a competitive market economy. That the Sherman Act and our other antitrust laws have not been fully successful in achieving this goal is generally acknowledged. Academic economists have been ready to blame this result on corrupt or inept public officials entrusted with enforcing these laws, an unenlightened judiciary, or, more generally, on the absence of any real constituency for maintaining an effectively competitive economy. Perhaps they are right. But economists must share the blame.

Although the antitrust laws were not enacted for economic reasons alone, their legal standards generally have been rooted more deeply in economics than in other systems of thought. So from the outset economic ideas of monopoly and competition played an important—though not always controlling—role in antitrust policy. But while economists were often asked to advise on these matters, they generally responded with little more than theories or opinions concerning the significance of alternative market structures. Most economists agreed that single-firm monopoly should not be tolerated, and therefore readily recommended that monopoly either be regulated or broken up. They likewise took an intolerant view toward restraints and combinations resulting in monopoly, but these areas of agreement provided little help in antitrust enforcement in a world composed almost exclusively of oligopolistic industries embracing a wide range of market concentration. There was no consensus among economists concerning the theoretical implications of oligopoly, much less reliable empirical evidence. As a result, the ad hoc speculations and empiricism of one economist was easily offset by that of another. Not too surprisingly, even the best intentioned public officials were more often confused than enlightened, despairing that economists would show them the truth. And the courts likely agreed with the observation of John Bates Clark over sixty years ago that "We certainly need to know more than that in its natural appearance, a trust resembles an octopus." As a result, the courts early turned to behavioral standards rooted more in business ethics than in economic empiricism.

The first breakthrough on the oligopoly front came with the pioneering theoretical works of the early 1930s, especially Edward Chamberlain's theory of monopolistic competition, which sought to explain gradations of market power that lay between perfect competition and absolute monopoly. The field of industrial organization grew out of these theoretical works of imperfect or monopolistic competition. Though these theories influenced antitrust policy, they failed to provide real coherence because the theories remained largely untested. Indeed, in 1942 no lesser economists than George Stigler believed that

"It is doubtful whether the monopoly question will ever receive much illumination from large-scale statistical investigation."[a]

In the early 1950s economists made the first faltering steps at statistical measurement of monopoly power. The initial tests were crude, based as they were on poor data and unsophisticated analytical techniques. And as late as 1960, economists still had not satisfactorily demonstrated empirically that market performance was greatly different at one level of concentration than another.

Over the last decade the number of empirical studies testing industrial organization hypotheses has grown from a trickle to a torrent, though for the most part they left much to be desired. This book is more than just another such study. Importantly, it demonstrates that the field of industrial organization lends itself to rigorous scientific analysis. Others have covered similar ground traveled by the authors. But the distinctive contribution of this study is its demonstration of the payoff from rigorous hypothesis formulation, careful data-gathering, and sophisticated application of statistical techniques. Others should learn from this example.

Although exercising the scientist's caution in not overstating their findings, industrial organization scholars will appreciate that this study seemingly has given the answer to some questions. Replication of their efforts is almost certain to bear out their finding that the higher the level of market concentration the higher the level of industry profits. This relationship comes through so strongly in all of their multiple regression equations that about the only open question, in my opinion, is whether this relationship is linear over the entire range of concentration, as they find over the range of their observations.

Although this study covers only one broad sector of the American economy—firms in the food and kindred products industries—it sheds considerable light on issues currently confronting those enforcing existing antitrust laws as well as legislators contemplating new legislation to cope with the "concentrated industries problem." Thirteen years ago, Edward S. Mason, the pioneer of the empirical study of industrial organization, wrote that there was an "element of faith" in the proposition that maintaining competition was desirable and that "a substantial amount of guesswork" was involved in identifying the extent of market power.[b] The authors of this research monograph have aided in reducing

---

[a] George Stigler, "The Extent and Bases of Monopoly," *American Economic Review*, XXXII, No. 2, Part 2, June 1942, pp. 1–22.
[b] In Carl Kaysen and Donald F. Turner, *Antitrust Policy*, Harvard University Press, 1959, p. xx.

the extent to which those responsible for public policy toward concentrated industries must rely on faith and guesswork.

Willard F. Mueller
Vilas Research Professor

Preface

There has developed in recent years a rather substantial interest in the estimation of relationships between market structure and market performance. The recent rate of growth in the amount of research in this area rivals that ordinarily ascribed to rabbits in a not unfriendly environment. Our main objective in contributing to this population explosion has been to estimate structure-performance relationships for the U.S. food processing sector using regression analysis and data for individual companies. This focus on the food sector, while somewhat narrow relative to many other researches, has allowed intensive study of important issues that have heretofore received scant attention. Where, for example, methods typically employed in industrial organization research have appeared to us to be inappropriate, we have striven to make whatever innovations our wits and resources would allow. On balance we hope that our book may prove to be rather like a mutation which, in another context, serves to improve the species in generations to come.

This book is the product of a joint venture which was conceived in 1967 at the University of Wisconsin. At that time both of the senior authors were graduate students in agricultural economics. They have since completed the requirements for the Ph.D. degree, and the present work is based in substantial measure on their dissertations. As to the division of labor among us, accountants and even some economists are aware that joint products often cause serious allocation problems; our joint effort is no exception to the rule. It would be disingenuous of us to attempt isolating where the work of one author begins and that of another ends. We choose not to try, except to note that the statistical models given in Chapter 2 are largely the creation of Blake Imel.

In the course of our endeavors, we have been assisted by many people. We would like to express our thanks to Willard F. Mueller, A. C. Johnson, Jr., and Reuben C. Buse for their many helpful comments. We would also like to express our appreciation to the executive personnel of the many companies who provided us with the data that made this study possible. The research was supported by the College of Agricultural and Life Sciences, University of Wisconsin, the Giannini Foundation, University of California, Berkeley, and the Marketing Economics Division, USDA. During the course of much of our research and during the writing of his Ph.D. thesis, Blake Imel was a USDA collaborator. We are solely responsible for any sins of omission or commission, and for these we beg for absolution.

Blake Imel
Michael R. Behr
Peter G. Helmberger

Introduction

The purpose of this monograph is to report the results of a research project in which the major objective was to estimate market structure-performance relationships for the food manufacturing sector of the United States. While market performance has many dimensions, our interest centers mainly on structure-profit rate relationships. An underlying premise is that such relationships have important implications for competition, which, in turn, has important implications for product-mix efficiency, that is, efficiency in the allocation of resources among competing products. Of secondary interest in this study is the relationship between structure and progressiveness. Performance dimensions other than product-mix efficiency and progressiveness are largely ignored.

Our research has been motivated by the continuing search for better information on structure-performance relationships and the belief that the methods and procedures commonly employed in this area of research could be improved. The importance of better information on structure-performance relationships need not detain us long here. At issue is the "monopoly problem," which has been a perpetual public concern. At present, significant government energies are expended through the Justice Department, Federal Trade Commission, and other Federal agencies, and state agencies too, in order to curb monopolistic activities in the marketplace. Aside from the value of testing price theory, a better knowledge of structure-performance relationships could have considerable practical significance in detecting monopoly power and in attacking its foundations through so-called structural remedies such as the dissolution of relatively large, oftentimes highly diversified firms. Without going into the merits of the case, the object of structural remedies is to establish structural conditions among industries in order to assure, through effective competition, acceptable or workable market performance without further governmental controls. A knowledge of the economic consequences of alternative market structures is obviously relevant to the application of such remedies.

Regarding the adequacy of research methods, several issues are explored in the narrative that follows. Many analysts have complained about the limitations of data available from secondary sources without, as in the case of the weather, ever doing much about it. The role of industry definitions in research and, particularly, the heavy reliance placed on the four-digit definitions provided by the Census have been of common concern. Perhaps of less concern but of equal import is the inadequate attention given to the theoretical foundations for estimation procedures and statistical tests that have been commonly employed in quantitative analysis. Regarding the appropriate level of aggregation— whether it is best in some sense to work with firms, industries, or sectors—there have been sharp differences in points of view. These and other issues encountered in industrial organization should make the research methodology described in this monograph of interest to researchers, quite aside from empirical findings.

For purposes of this monograph, the food manufacturing sector is defined to include companies primarily engaged in food and kindred products, Census Group 20, and in tobacco manufacturing, Census Group 21. The decision to study only one segment of manufacturing reflected our desire to concentrate our efforts rather than spreading them over the entire manufacturing sector. The food sector was chosen because of our familiarity with it and in light of the agricultural orientation of our financial sponsors. Moreover, the food sector offers a wide variety of structural settings, and the fact that much of its output is distributed through the same wholesaling-retailing distribution system might tend to lessen the chances of error caused by our neglect of the structures of procurement industries. It might be worth noting that the food sector represents a sizable share of the total manufacturing sector, accounting, in 1967, for 11% of all value added by manufacturing and about the same percentage of the total number of establishments.

A generalized least squares regression model is used to measure the impact of structural and other explanatory variables upon the rates of profit and rates of research and development expenditures of the large food processing companies. The sensitivity of the regression results to different statistical models and different sets of industry definitions is analyzed. A major conclusion is that concentration, product differentiation, and barriers to entry are important variables in explaining the variation among rates of return for sample companies. The evidence for concentration is particularly compelling and suggests that the manner in which industries are defined may have substantial influence on statistical results. These conclusions are not unqualified, however, and the sensitivity analysis is of considerable interest. Also, with respect to rates of return, it developed that absolute size of firm, plant scale barriers to entry, market growth, and diversification variables produced estimated coefficients occasionally with unexpected signs and most often with low levels of statistical significance.

Turning to progressiveness, where our findings are more tentative, concentration and diversification appear to be positively related to rates of research and development expenditures. Product differentiation and absolute firm size appear not to be significant variables. Again, as in the case of profits, the results concerning concentration are sensitive to market definition and tend to be stronger the more theoretically justifiable the definitions.

The nature of methodological innovations contained in this monograph can conveniently be conveyed through describing briefly its organization. Attention is first focused on a statement of the industrial organization (IO) framework in which are traced out the correspondences between the constructs of price theory and empirical observations. Our rendition of the IO framework gives emphasis to categories of determinants of market performance other than those traditionally emphasized in the structure-performance scheme. Given this framework, conceptual and empirical issues associated with earlier cross section statistical studies are reviewed, and some of the resulting observations have important implications for our statistical and empirical findings.

Attention is then centered on estimation procedures. Considering a regression equation with profit rates for individual companies as the dependent variable, the error or disturbance term is broken up into component parts, each part attributable to the omission of a different category of explanatory variables. Theoretical analysis of the component error term leads to important a priori conclusions. A pattern of heteroskedasticity is predicted in the variance-covariance matrix for the error term. On the basis of this result, the problem of heteroskedastic regression residuals encountered previously by Hall and Weiss, the Federal Trade Commission, and others who have used classical least squares estimation procedures could have been anticipated.[1] As one might have expected, company diversification is the root cause of the difficulty. It is also shown that the error term in the true relationship is characterized by a predictable pattern of autocorrelation if more than one firm is included from any one industry. As a consequence of a heteroskedastic autocorrelated disturbance term, classical least squares regression is not an appropriate estimation procedure where there is an interest in using tests of statistical significance. Generalized least squares is required if the object is minimum variance linear unbiased estimates. Unfortunately, straightforward application of generalized least squares regression is not possible without a knowledge of the ratios of certain population variances. In our quantitative work we have had to make do with ad hoc procedures and analyses of the sensitivity of empirical results to alternative statistical specifications.

In light of the shortcomings of available data, an effort was made to collect relevant information in a field survey. A short chapter describes this survey, which involved personal interviews with executives from leading companies across the nation as well as telephone interviews and mailed questionnaires. One objective was to collect information on variables that are often excluded from analysis for want of necessary data. Company interviews were also very useful in framing three alternative sets of industry definitions used in assessing the impacts of differing definitions on statistical estimates. In addition, our estimation procedures could never have been implemented in the absence of primary data collected in the survey.

Our major statistical findings for rates of profit are given in Chapter 5 and those for progressiveness are given in Chapter 6. Chapter 7 spells out the implications of our analysis of component error terms for various levels of aggregation in cross-section research. A general conclusion is that the effects of aggregation may not be as clear-cut as has previously been thought. A summary and some further interpretations of our findings are given in Chapter 8

1 The Economic Framework and Some Problems of Application

The economic framework for this monograph comprehends pretty much the entire body of price theory plus a number of observations aimed at augmenting that theory in light of some of its more embarrassing oversimplifications. It would be patently inappropriate to attempt a complete summary of price theory here but a brief discussion of some definitions and hypotheses will help set the stage for the later development of an econometric model and an empirical application of that model in estimating structure-performance relationships in the food sector.

It is instructive to begin by giving a quick definition of a selling industry, postponing until later the practical problems of application. A *selling industry* may be defined as a group of firms selling products that are viewed as close substitutes by a common group of buyers. If any one buyer is completely indifferent between the product of any one seller and the product of any other, the products may be said to be perfect substitutes. It is unnecessary that the substitutes be perfect, however. Some buyers might be willing to pay a modest price premium for the product of a certain seller while others might buy the product only at par or even at a discount. It is also to be understood that the product of any one seller in an industry is, relatively, a distant substitute for the product of a seller in any other industry. Clearly, a diversified firm may be a seller in many industries. Presumably, then, the products must perform similar functions for buyers (sugar can be used to sweeten foods and beverages) and the sellers and buyers must be in the same spatial-temporal area in light of transportation and storage costs. Bread bakers in San Francisco do not compete with bakers in New York. Early California plum producers do not compete with late plum producers.

A *market* may be defined to include a selling industry plus the buyers of the substitute products in question. It consists of more than an aggregate of buyers and sellers in that the existence of certain exchange expectations and traditions that relate buyers and sellers together is presupposed.

A question of central importance in this monograph is: What determines the level of competition among sellers in a market? This immediately raises the issue of the meaning of that rather elusive term "competition." It is helpful to consider two polar cases. In the case of perfect competition, firms have no leeway whatsoever in assigning values to the variables that determine the firm's long-run profit. The firm has no influence over price. It must choose the best technology, combine inputs in optimal proportions, and produce a certain level of output under the pain of bankruptcy. The market dictates what the firm must do in order to survive. The firm is utterly without power. The pure monopolist, at the other extreme, may well have the power to set price, with considerable latitude over levels of cost or internal efficiency. In this case, the market places some constraints on profit decisions but there may be many alternative courses of action open to him, each consistent with survival.

A well-known theorem of price theory states that maximization of industry profit, monopolization, calls for equating the industry marginal cost of production to the industry marginal revenue from the sale of the output. The potential payoff from monopolization is extant in every market. That is to say, if marginal revenue does not equal marginal cost, industry profit may be increased through either a small increase or a small decrease in output. Except in the case of monopoly, however, no firm will have complete control over industry marginal revenue or cost, and to assure the appropriate equality requires that sellers coordinate their behavior. The degree of competition in a market refers to the extent to which competing sellers coordinate their profit policies in order to garner some, if not all, of the fruits of monopoly.

In identifying the determinants of competition, it is worth noting that microeconomic theory is constructed through characterizing economic agents by assumption, placing these agents in theoretical environments, and then conducting intellectual experiments in which decision making and the associated consequences are predicted in light of assumed changes in the environment. Obviously, the predictions of price theory rest in no small way on the assumption that economic agents are maximizers. The behavioralists have repeatedly stressed the possibility that theoretical predictions might go awry because human decision making is far more complex than the maximizing postulate would have us believe. This is perhaps particularly true in the case of the firm where the large modern corporation stands in sharp contrast to profit-maximizing entrepreneurs.

As applied to the problem at hand, there is a very great likelihood that the organizational characteristics of large corporations, such as the degree of centralization or the identity of major goal-setters, will have substantial impact on the competition among them. As Mason argued many years ago, "firms are not, regardless of what economic theory may suppose, undifferentiated, profit-maximizing agencies which react to given market situations in ways which are independent of their organization."[1] In spite of Mason's early caveat, IO researchers have given short shrift to the impacts of organizational variables on the levels of competition and the behavioralists seem to have been interested mainly in other matters.[2]

But let us take the organizational characteristics of firms as given, not bothering to consider how such characteristics get determined. A major thrust of price theory is that the nature of the market environment itself may have an important bearing on the competitiveness of sellers. In this connection, *market structure* may be defined as the set of environmental elements that, given the organizational characteristics of sellers, determines the degree of seller competition. Structural dimensions receiving the greatest attention in the literature are buyer and seller concentration, product differentiation, and barriers to entry. The list can be expanded considerably, however, if one is willing to use ad hoc theoretical arguments. In addition, it need not be supposed that an environmental element that is a part of structure in one market is a part of structure in all other markets. Thus, for example, we would expect independent conduct where market structure is atomistic regardless of the degree of demand elasticity, but elasticity might be an important part of structure in oligopolistic markets.[3] While undoubtedly helpful in identifying environmental elements that determine the competitiveness of sellers, price theory is particularly weak in the very case, oligopoly, that we have come to believe is the most prevalent in the real world. There is little doubt but what the present state of "oligopoly theory" places a heavy burden on empirical research aimed at identifying and measuring the importance of structural elements.

The competitiveness of sellers in a market would appear to be of some considerable significance, and therefore worthy of study, in that it determines the extent to which market performance departs from that which we would expect given perfectly competitive behavior. In static partial equilibrium formulations, market performance consists of the levels of industry output and per-unit cost of production. Taking dynamic and other considerations into account, investment levels, progressiveness in terms of new product and process development, the range of product qualities open to buyers, conservation of natural resources, and the extent and nature of promotional programs would also appear to be of great importance.

Given the manner in which firms coordinate their behavior—that is, the degree of competition—market performance depends on technological relationships, prices of inputs, demand conditions, uncertainty, the information available to buyers and sellers, and the like. We will refer to these latter categories of data as *basic economic data*. The degree of competition, then, does not determine market performance per se. Rather, given basic economic data, it determines the departure from that expected in competitive equilibrium or under pure monopoly. This is important because in empirical research we can observe performance directly but can only estimate, in most cases at least, what the competitive (monopolistic) outcome would be.

We may now briefly summarize the industrial organizational framework as envisaged in the above remarks. Given the organizational characteristics of firms, market structure determines the competitiveness of sellers, which determines, in light of basic economic data, market performance. An example might add concreteness. Two profit-maximizing duopolists in a blockaded industry might decide to engage in perfect collusion in light of the obvious interdependency. Actual decisions regarding levels of output would doubtless vary over time in light of changes in demand, technology, and input prices. The resulting pattern of observed market performance would reflect not only structure, which merely led to collusion, but also the goals of the duopolists and the changes in basic economic data. As to applications of this framework, Scherer, in his study of the determinants of industrial progressiveness, considers both the structures of industries and their differing opportunities for research and development activities. Such opportunities would be classified as part of basic economic data in our terminology. Kamerschen sought to relate company profit rates to both the nature of company ownership and control of the structure of the market in which the company operates; thus, obviously giving attention to the organized characteristics of the firm. [4]

The flow of causality assumed in this framework is unilateral, flowing from structure to performance. In a dynamic context it is realized that competitive behavior and performance at one point in time might determine, or at least influence, market structure in subsequent periods. The general concensus seems to be, however, that organizational characteristics of firms and market structure, especially in the case of mature industries, tend to be relatively stable over time; short-run changes in performance are due mainly to changes in basic economic data.

Price theory has more to say, however, than simply that structure determines performance in light of certain "givens"; there is a strong suggestion from the various structural models that the closer market structure is to that associated with perfect competition (pure monopoly) the closer market performance is to the perfectly competitive (monopolistic) outcome. Though performance is multidimensional, this basic structural hypothesis pertains mainly to the implications of alternative market structures for the allocation of resources among competing products. In perfect competition, production in the various industries is pushed to the point where industry marginal cost is equated to price. When competition is less than perfect, because of implicit or explicit collusive agreements, we would expect industry price-marginal cost gaps to occur as firms restricted output below the competitive level in order to bring industry marginal cost and marginal revenue into equality.

A simple hypothetical example might help explain both the nature and the consequence of monopoly pricing. The quantities of products A and B are plotted on the vertical and horizontal axes, respectively, in Figure 1-1. The curve labeled T is a product transformation function showing the maximum quantities of A and B that can be produced with a given batch of productive inputs. Assume B is produced by a pure monopolist and A by a perfectly competitive industry; the slope of line L is determined by the ratio of the price of B to the price of A. Final equilibrium is at P where society is on the product transformation curve and all productive services are employed. Let I represent the indifference curve for the ith consumer. In equilibrium, the consumer is, of course, equating the price ratio to the ratios of his marginal utilities. Notice, however, that it would be possible to make the ith consumer better off by producing more of B and less of A without making any other consumer worse off. (See point H, for example.)

ECONOMIC FRAMEWORK AND SOME PROBLEMS OF APPLICATION 9

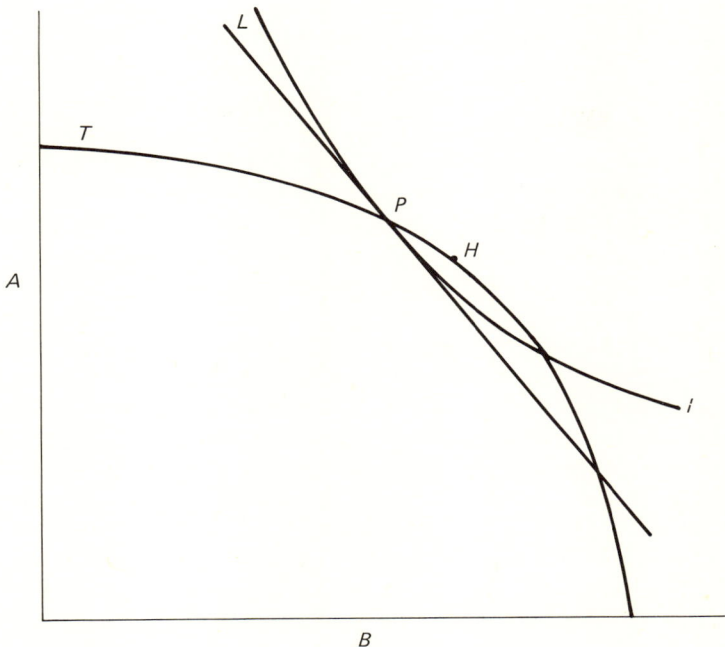

Figure 1-1. Equilibrium given a monopolized industry producing product B and a competitive industry producing product A.

Had there been perfect competition in both industries, the price line would have been tangent to the product transformation curve; it would have been impossible to make any consumer better off without making some other consumer worse off. In a word, monopoly gives rise to the "wrong" product mix in that consumers would be better off at some other point on the transformation function.

Aside from the allocation of inputs among competing products, the basic structural hypothesis has little to say regarding other dimensions of performance. With regard to wasteful and deceptive promotional programs, the appropriate theoretical model would need assume imperfect information on the part of decision makers, a model that economists are generally loathe to analyze. Profit maximization implies that the cost of production would be minimized regardless of the level of output. Regarding progressiveness, price theory is statical and takes as given the products to be produced, the inputs to be used, and the technological relationships which link inputs and products together; little is offered in the way of a priori associations between market structure and progressiveness.

Given the hypotheses flowing out of price theory and their relevance to public policy, the need for empirical research is evident. There is the question whether the hypotheses are in accord in some acceptable manner with observation. In light of the qualitative nature of the hypotheses, there is the quite obvious need for quantifying any relationships that might, in fact, exist. In addition, it is quite possible that price theory may ignore important variables and relationships which might go undetected in the absence of empirical research.

In attempting to establish empirical links between competitiveness of sellers and structural situations, it is unfortunately very difficult to measure directly the degree of competition among sellers in an industry and to make interindustry comparisons. For one thing, antitrust laws make certain types of noncompetitive behavior illegal, and the economist is confronted with the unenviable task of studying the behavior of intelligent guinea pigs who may be quite anxious to befuddle those seeking to describe and elucidate their behavior. Of likely greater importance, however, is the fact that our perception of the meaning of competition among sellers is simply not sufficiently precise to allow direct measurement. Without such measurements, direct comparisons among the levels of competition in industries representing a variety of structural situations are not possible.

But all is not lost, for we would expect that the degree of competition would manifest itself in the extent of company profits, and profits *can* be observed. More specifically, as competition tends toward the monopolistic extreme, we would, *ceteris paribus,* expect the rate of profit to increase also. This immediately suggests correlating structure with profit rates as a means for revealing associations between structure and competition.

It is worth emphasizing that profit per se is not an element of performance. But where excess profit can be linked empirically with monopoly elements, there is the presumption on the basis of theoretical arguments adduced above that the allocation of resources among competing products is not optimal from the viewpoint of consumer welfare. There is the presumption that some products, those produced in industries characterized by monopoly elements, are produced in insufficient quantities relative to other products. Assuming constant marginal costs, the ratio of economic profit to sales measures the ratio of price minus marginal cost to price. If the price-marginal cost ratio in industry A exceeds the corresponding ratio in industry B, a small transfer of resources—say a dollar's worth—from B to A would, in the absence of externalities, likely increase consumer welfare.

At this juncture it is convenient to reemphasize that the relationship between structure and profit in the food processing sector is of major interest in this research. Considering performance, we are interested mainly in efficiency in the allocation of resources among competing products. Other elements of market performance, except for progressiveness, are ignored. Our treatment of progressiveness is motivated primarily by Schumpeter, Galbraith, and others who argue that big business and/or monopoly power are conducive to the growth of new products and processes and innovation generally. A more careful statement of the Schumpeterian and neo-Schumpeterian hypotheses will be given later in connection with our empirical work. It should be noted further that our analysis of progressiveness is relatively tentative and exploratory in nature.

It would be beyond the scope of this monograph to offer a critical survey of all quantitative research on structure-performance relationships. It is useful, however, in light of subsequent analysis, to note certain general difficulties encountered in such studies. While discussion of these difficulties focuses on profit rates, many of the conclusions reached are applicable as well to progressiveness.

Much of the earlier research on the structure-profit relationship dealt with aggregates of firms, grouped to represent industries or aggregates of industries.[5] In many cases, the method of classical least squares (CLS) was used to estimate a hypothesized population function of the form:

$$R_i = a + \sum_{j=1}^{J} b_{ij} X_{ij} + u_i \qquad (1.1)$$

where

R_i = the ratio of profit to sales (or to some measure of capital), say for the ith group of firms, $i = 1, \ldots, n$.

X_{ij} = the jth structural variable, a concentration ratio for example, for the ith group of firms, $j = 1, \ldots, J$.

u_i = the stochastic error term for the ith group.

Implicit in the interpretation of the results of many of these studies has been the assumption that the error term, u_i, possesses certain desirable statistical properties. The validity of these assumptions, as they relate to group studies, will be scrutinized at a later point.

Estimation of the parameters of Equation (1.1) entails the empirical delineation of industries, and herein lies one of the major difficulties in industrial organization research. Researchers have relied heavily on census definitions of industries even though the census and economic criteria for industry definition differ substantially. There are probably two reasons for this reliance. Obviously, one is the comprehensive information on concentration available for various industrial groupings defined by the census. Another is that it is much easier for a researcher to use census definitions than to apply fuzzy economic criteria in establishing his own. Be that as it may, the issue arises whether empirical results are sensitive to industry definition and we shall have more to say later on this subject.

A second difficulty concerns the estimation of a meaningful rate of profit for each industry or group of industries, given that many corporations are highly diversified. The returns of these companies reflect the conditions in more than one industry and the problem is essentially one of matching appropriate dependent and independent variables. For discussion, it is convenient to distinguish between an industry approach and a sector approach.

In the industry approach, researchers attempt to compute rates of profit for industries, which are then correlated with structural elements. One method of estimating industry profit rates is through aggregation of profits of leading firms from each industry, excluding those firms that are heavily diversified.[6] Avoiding these firms will not only limit the choice of firms within each industry, but in some cases may limit the industries that can be represented. Also, it would appear impossible to completely avoid all diversification and maintain much of a sample. Another method of arriving at an industry profit rate entails the use of value added and other census data that have been collected at the plant level and classified by four-digit industry [7] The resulting margins are not adjusted for payments to capital or product promotion expenditures, both of which are conceivably correlated with certain elements of market structure. There are other objections to the method that need not detain us here.

The second approach, involving analysis of industry aggregates, takes the combined financial data of all firms that are primarily engaged in one of several related industries and attempts to match structural data to the resulting rate of profit.[8] More specifically, the profit rate for each observation represents a weighted average for all firms that are primarily engaged in a single Standard Industrial Classification (SIC) two-digit major group or Internal Revenue Service (IRS) minor industry. Either one of these groups corresponds to a collection of SIC four-digit industries, the latter being taken most often as the best approximation to theoretical industries. The structural variables for each of these broader aggregates are computed by taking weighted averages of the structural variables of the component four-digit industries, using four-digit sales or assets as weights. On the assumption that the sales of the companies included in each SIC major group or IRS minor industry account for the total population sales of each component four-digit group and nothing else, the problems of diversification are overcome and the rationale of the procedure can easily be demonstrated.

Assume that Markets 1 and 2 make up the Tth sector. The sales in these markets are S_1 and S_2, respectively, while profits (after all payments to capital) are P_1 and P_2. Following the notation used in Equation (1.1):

$$R_i = \frac{P_i}{S_i} = a + BX_{ij} + u_i, \quad i = 1, 2 \tag{1.2}$$

so that:

$$P_i = (a + BX_{ij} + u_i)S_i, \quad i = 1, 2 \tag{1.3}$$

ECONOMIC FRAMEWORK AND SOME PROBLEMS OF APPLICATION

By definition:

$$P_1 + P_2 = P_T, \quad S_1 + S_2 = S_T$$

so that:

$$R_T = \frac{P_1 + P_2}{S_1 + S_2}$$

$$= a + B\left(\frac{S_1}{S_T}X_{1j} + \frac{S_2}{S_T}X_{2j}\right) + \frac{S_1}{S_T}u_1 + \frac{S_2}{S_T}u_2 \qquad (1.4)$$

The ratios of market-to-sector sales, S_1/S_T and S_2/S_T in this case, are in fact the sort of weights that have been applied to independent variables in analysis of aggregates.

If the initial assumptions of the above approach are not met, however—and they strictly imply that no firm is ever diversified beyond its primary SIC two-digit group or IRS minor industry—the analysis is in error. Blair's analysis of 1963 Census data for the 200 largest manufacturing companies shows that, on the average, only about 17% of these firms which operated a plant in any given SIC two-digit group were also primarily engaged in that group.[9] This is only a rough indicator of a potential problem, of course, The real issue turns on the importance of nonprimary activities in distorting the aggregate profit rate, or from another view, the weighted independent variables. Distortion, of course, depends upon the relative magnitudes of nonprimary activities rather than only their incidence. It should be noted that the IRS groups are more narrowly defined than the SIC two-digit groups and would, therefore, be more susceptible to errors due to diversification.

Turning to the third difficulty, Bain, apparently an advocate of the single industry approach, has severely criticized the sector grouping procedure on different grounds. He argues that grouping by sector will suppress the interindustry variance in both structural variables and profits, thereby obscuring the relationship.[10] While the argument may have theoretical merit, the question it poses is essentially empirical. Stigler and Collins and Preston,[11] among others, have noted that the observed relationship between the rate of return and one major structural variable, concentration, tends to be stronger where the level of aggregation is higher. Bain himself notes the relative strength of results from one analysis of two-digit groups.[12] An intuitive explanation may be that the grouping tends to dampen the unexplainable variance relative to the explainable, a possibility not considered by Bain. The matter may not be so straightforward as previously supposed, however, and discussion of this third problem—the potential effects of aggregation—is reserved until subsequent theoretical arguments can be brought to bear on the issue.

Before turning to the fourth difficulty, it is convenient to note that in contrast to market and sector studies, several more recent researches have sought to explain the variation among the rates of return for individual companies.[13] That is to say, the dependent variable of Equation (1.1) represents the returns of a single firm, and included among the independent variables are structural variables for the markets in which the particular firm is engaged. Conceptually, and disregarding data problems, these micro analyses would appear to be more illuminating than the more aggregative approaches. Industry performance is nothing more or less than the aggregate of firm performance. Explaining the variance among profit rates of firms taken from a cross-section of industries would yield, as a by-product, an explanation of variance among industry profit rates.

In addition, variance in the profit rates among firms within an industry is of intrinsic interest. A price-marginal cost gap for an industry must be viewed as a weighted average of gaps for its component firms. Variation in such gaps among firms within an industry may be as important to resource allocation as variation among industries. Take an example. It should be quite evident that the degree of product differentiation varies greatly among the firms in an industry. The food sector is rife with examples of industries in which some firms produce mainly for private labels while others produce mainly for national brand markets. Within an industry one might well seek to determine the extent to which a firm differentiates its product from the products of others and with what consequence for its rate of profit. Using industry averages conceals potentially important variance in both the dependent and the independent variables. How such variation should be handled within analyses of company profit data poses serious problems, as we shall see.

It is instructive to pursue this problem further in light of a classification of variables considered below. Suppose that advertising expenditures expressed as a percentage of sales is adopted as a measure of the degree of product differentiation. With company profit rate as the dependent variable, the researcher might include the industry level of advertising as a percentage of sales as an independent variable and the firm's deviation from the industry level as another. Abstracting from other determinants of profit rates, if all firms in an industry have the same rates of advertising expenditures, we would expect similar profit rates. (These rates might exceed competitive levels because the uniform rates of advertising might give rise to a barrier to entry.)

Implicit in our suggestion for handling product differentiation in analyzing variance among company profit rates is the notion of a variable that affects the profit of one firm but which has no effect on the profits of others—for instance, the deviation of the firm's advertising rate from the industry level. We will refer to such variables as *firm variables*. Firm variables may take on unique values for and have unique impacts on a firm's profit rate. They may be contrasted with *market variables,* in our parlance, that are assumed to affect all firms in the same manner. Published research contains many suggested examples of firm variables. The FTC study included firm diversification and firm size as independent variables. Kamerschen included independent variables that reflected the company's organizational characteristics, as previously noted. As another potentially important example, the quality of a firm's management relative to the average managerial ability for the industry might tend to affect the firm's profit with little or no effect on profits of the other firms.

It is our impression that insufficient attention has been given in previous work to the role of firm-related variables in profit determination. A potentially serious complication arises out of the possibility that firm-related variables may tend to be of much greater importance in determining profit rates in atomistic industries than in highly concentrated industries where all firms are caught up in a tight web of interdependency. Subsequent analysis focuses to a rather limited extent on this particular issue, however.

A fourth problem that is perhaps particularly bothersome in analyses of company profit rates, though it may appear in more aggregative studies too, concerns heteroskedasticity. When classical least squares is used to explain variation among profit rates of individual companies, heteroskedasticity is frequently detected in the residuals. It has been recognized that company diversification might be the root cause of this problem in firm studies though attempts to deal with the problem have involved examination of the residuals and ad hoc weighting schemes based on the sizes of firms.[14] In the model given below, we suggest a method for dealing with problems of heteroskedasticity based in large measure on a priori theoretical considerations and in which diversification plays a key role. We also give attention to another statistical problem, autocorrelation, which has previously gone unnoticed in this area of work.

A fifth problem has to do with the adequacy of the partial equilibrium approach, with its emphasis on single-product firms, in dealing with the complex phenomenon of diversification and conglomeration. Grether has recently written "the most important issue for the field of industrial organization is how to bring the large diversified corporation within the framework of analysis."[15] A very simple approach supposes that the diversified firm is a mere aggregate of "single-product firms" or divisions, each of which is subject to independent structural analysis. The emphasis on performance at the level of the division is quite in keeping with price theory's emphasis on industry price-marginal cost gaps, though few would argue that viewing the diversified firm as a mere aggregate is realistic. What commends this approach is its operationality. Profit of the company, which is observable, is viewed as a sum of the profits of divisions and is written as a function of weighted independent variables. This approach will be given a rigorous development in the econometric formulation given below.

We recognize, however, that the diversified company may cause new and serious problems in that it may amount to a good deal more than a simple aggregate of specialized "firms." Not only might it become more difficult to measure the traditional variables, but new variables may need to be included in the analysis. There may be spillover effects in differentiating products in the various markets. There may be complementaries in multiple-product production. To the extent Edwards is correct in emphasizing forebearance among conglomerates, for example, additional structural variables may be needed to reflect the extent of conglomerate operations in the various markets. While these are important issues, they will not receive much attention in what follows.

2 Estimation Procedures

Having assayed briefly the theoretical underpinnings of market structure-performance relationships and having noted some general difficulties in quantitative research, we now turn to the matter of an appropriate estimation procedure given observations on individual firms rather than on industries or sectors. It is argued on a priori grounds that omission of independent variables leads to heteroskedastic and autocorrelated disturbance terms and that generalized least squares (*GLS*) is a prerequisite for efficient estimates of population parameters and meaningful tests of significance. By implication, classical least squares (*CLS*) would not appear to be an appropriate estimation procedure where there is an interest in using statistical tests. The treatment of econometric problems is not intended to be comprehensive, however, in that many sources of specification error, such as errors in the variables, are not analyzed. Treatment of specification error can be readily found elsewhere.

It is instructive to begin by considering a world which is much simpler than the one we know in that all firms are completely specialized single-market firms. Suppose further that a researcher selects a random sample of firms which, fortuitously, just happens to contain no more than one firm in any one industry. With the resulting survey data, classical least squares regression might be employed to estimate the parameters of the following equation:

$$R_{ij} = a + bM_j + cE_{ij} + u_{ij} \qquad (2.1)$$

where

R_{ij} = the ratio of economic profit to sales (or some measure of capital) of the ith firm operating in the jth industry.

M_j = a market-related structural variable, such as a concentration ratio, which is common to all firms in the jth industry.

E_{ij} = a firm-related variable, such as quality of management (or the degree of product differentiation enjoyed) relative to the industry average, for the ith firm in the jth industry,

u_{ij} = an error term resulting from the omission of independent (both firm and market) variables.[1]

If $E(u_{ij}) = 0$, if $E(u_{ij} u_{kh}) = \sigma_u^2$ when both $i = k$ and $j = h$, and 0 otherwise; and if the error term is uncorrelated with the included independent variables, the estimates of the parameters a, b, and c will have certain desirable properties. Moreover, statistical tests of significance are available if the error term u_{ij} is normally distributed. All of these assumptions concerning the error component appear reasonable under these controlled conditions. There are potential difficulties, however, when the sample contains more than one firm from any one industry and where some firms are diversified. Each of these complications is taken up in turn.

Model I: Specialized Firm Model

It is, of course, quite possible that a random sample of specialized firms could contain a number of firms from any one industry. To see the resulting implications for the properties of the error term, it is instructive to split that term, u_{ij}, into two components:

$$u_{ij} = e_{ij} + m_j \qquad (2.2)$$

where e_{ij} is that portion of the total error term attributable to omission of firm-related variables and m_j equals the error due to the omission of market-related variables. In the light of the available data and the complexity of the real world, it appears almost certain that many independent variables—some market-related and some firm-related—will usually be omitted in empirical work.

The decomposition of the error term into two components is consistent with the previous formulation, Equation (2.1), if the error components have the following sufficient properties:

$E(e_{ij}) = E(m_j) = 0$

$E(e_{ij} e_{kh}) = 0$ where either $i \neq k$ or $j \neq h$

$E(e_{ij} m_k) = 0$ where $j \neq k$

$E(m_j m_h) = 0$ where $j \neq h$

Furthermore, by definition, omission of market-related variables leads to an m_j which is identical for all firms in industry j, so that $C(e_{ij}, m_j) = 0$. Appealing to the central limits theorem, we can assume that both m_j and e_{ij} are normally distributed with a finite variance.[2]

ESTIMATION PROCEDURES

With these specifications in mind, let us return to Equation (2.1) where j ranges over $1 \ldots m$ markets and i may range over $1 \ldots n$ firms although it is to be understood that the number of firms in each industry may vary. The variance-covariance matrix of u_{ij}, hereafter referred to as the *omega matrix*, will be examined in more detail. The diagonal term is given by:

$$V(u_{ij}) = V(e_{ij}) + V(m_j) + 2\,C(e_{ij}, m_j)$$
$$= \sigma_e^2 + \sigma_m^2 + 0 \tag{2.3}$$

Turning to the covariance between u_{ij} and u_{kh}, the error terms for two different firms, we have:

$$C(u_{ij}\, u_{kh}) = E(u_{ij}\, u_{kh}) + E(u_{ij})\, E(u_{kh})$$
$$= E[(m_j + e_{ij})(m_h + e_{kh})]$$
$$= E(m_j\, m_h)$$
$$= \begin{cases} \sigma_m^2 & \text{if } j = h \\ 0 & \text{if } j \neq h \end{cases} \tag{2.4}$$

If two firms operate in the same market, they have the same m_j submerged in their error terms; the expected cross product of the two m_j's is σ_m^2. The expectation of the remainder of the cross products, including the cross products of the m_j's for the two firms not in the same market, equals zero by assumption. The emergence of a positive off-diagonal element (wherever two firms are in the same market) in the omega matrix means that classical least squares is no longer appropriate.

Summarizing the above derivations in terms of matrix notation will facilitate comparisons between this and other models. We will hereafter refer to the ratio $K = \sigma_m^2 / \sigma_u^2$ as the *omega ratio*. Let U equal the $n \times 1$ column vector of u_{ij}'s associated with the n firms in the sample. Then we have:

$$E(U\,U') = \sigma_u^2\, \Omega_1,$$

where:

$$\Omega_1 = \begin{bmatrix} 1 & 0 & 0 & K & . & . & . & 0 & . & . & . & K \\ 0 & 1 & K & 0 & & & & & & & & \\ 0 & K & 1 & 0 & & & & & & & & \\ K & 0 & 0 & 1 & & & & & & & & \\ . & & & & . & & & & & & & \\ . & & & & & & & & & & & \\ . & & & & & & & & & & & \\ & 0 & & & & & & 1 & & & & \\ . & & & & & & & & & & & \\ . & & & & & & & & & & & \\ . & & & & & & & & & & & \\ K & & & & & & & & & & & 1 \end{bmatrix}$$

Given any two firms, the corresponding element in the omega matrix equals K if the firms are in the same industry, and zero otherwise. The pattern of zero's and K's partly specified in the above matrix is illustrative only. Apparently the first, fourth, and nth firms are in the same industry. The second and third firms are both in a different industry. (Only if $E(U\,U')$ equaled $\sigma^2 I$, where I is the $n \times n$ identity matrix, would CLS be an appropriate estimation procedure.)

Model II: The Diversified Firm, First Approximation

We turn next to a more complex diversified firm model world in which at least some of the firms may be diversified. It is assumed that a diversified firm is nothing more or less than an aggregate of single-product firms (each of which will be referred to as a division) so that all our assumptions about the relationships of the various components of the error term still apply. Obviously this is but an approximation of the real world, and the general model discussed below is intended as a more realistic formulation.

Consider, then, the profit function of the tth and kth firms given below where P equals the level of profit and S the level of sales:

$$P_{tj} = (a + bM_j + cE_{tj} + e_{tj} + m_j) S_{tj} \tag{2.5}$$

$$P_{kh} = (a + bM_h + cE_{kh} + e_{kh} + m_h) S_{kh} \tag{2.6}$$

The ith diversified firm, on the other hand, which consists of these two "firms" or divisions would have the following profit rate function:

$$R_{id} = a + b(D_{ij}M_j + D_{ih}M_h) + c(D_{ij}E_{tj} + D_{ih}E_{kh})$$
$$+ D_{ij}(e_{tj} + m_j) + D_{ih}(e_{kh} + m_h) \tag{2.7}$$

ESTIMATION PROCEDURES

where:

R_{id} = the ratio of total profit, P_{id}, to total sales, S_{id}, for the ith diversified firm,

D_{ij} = the share of the diversified firm's total sales accounted for by its sales in the jth market,

D_{ih} = the share of the diversified firm's total sales accounted for by its sales in the hth market.

Equation (2.7) shows the necessity of using weighted independent variables in regression analysis of diversified firms, a suggestion that is scarcely new. It is analogous to the weighting of market-related variables for the multimarket sector analysis described in the previous chapter. Note further that profit was expressed as a percentage of sales. Had profit been expressed relative to, say, assets (equity) the appropriate weights would have been changed correspondingly to the percentages of assets (equity) accounted for by the various divisions. As a practical matter, however, it would appear very difficult to allocate assets and impossible to allocate net worth among the various divisions of a diversified firm.

The error term from Equation (2.7) is rather complex and merits further attention. Let g_{id} equal the total error term for the ith diversified firm. It can be shown that the expectation of g_{id} equals zero:

$$E(g_{id}) = E[D_{ij}(e_{tj} + m_j) + D_{ih}(e_{kh} + m_h)]$$
$$= D_{ij}E(e_{tj}) + D_{ij}E(m_j) + D_{ih}E(e_{kh}) + D_{ih}E(m_h)$$
$$= 0 \qquad (2.8)$$

Turning to the variance of g_{id}, we have:

$$V(g_{id}) = E(g_{id}^2) - [E(g_{id})]^2$$
$$= E[D_{ij}(e_{tj} + m_j) + D_{ih}(e_{kh} + m_h)]^2 \qquad (2.9)$$

Expanding and taking expectations of individual terms leads to the following result:

$$V(g_{id}) = (D_{ij}^2 + D_{ih}^2)\sigma_u^2 \qquad (2.10)$$

These results can be generalized for any diversified firm. If the ith firm had operated in all m markets, for example:

$$V(g_{id}) = \sum_{j=1}^{m} D_{ij}^2 \sigma_u^2, \quad j = 1, \ldots, j, \ldots, h, \ldots, m. \qquad (2.11)$$

Turning to the off-diagonal elements of the omega matrix, consider, in addition to the ith diversified firm described above, the rth firm which operates the pth division in market j and the qth division in market s. Then,

$$C(g_{id}g_{rd}) = E(g_{id}g_{rd}) - E(g_{id})E(g_{rd})$$

$$= E[D_{ij}(e_{tj} + m_j) + D_{ih}(e_{kh} + m_h)] \cdot [D_{rj}(e_{pj} + m_j) +$$

$$D_{rs}(e_{qs} + m_s)] \quad (2.12)$$

Expanding and taking expectations of the individual terms, we have:

$$C(g_{id}g_{rd}) = D_{ij}D_{rj}\sigma_m^2 \quad (2.13)$$

The cross-product of market-related error terms gives rise to a positive relationship between the error terms of two firms sharing at least one market. If two firms, whether specialized or diversified, share no market, the corresponding covariance term equals zero. If our ith and rth diversified firms had shared, say, z markets, then,

$$C(g_{id}g_{rd}) = \sum_{j=1}^{z} D_{ij}D_{rj}\sigma_m^2, \quad j = 1, \ldots, j, \ldots, z. \quad (2.14)$$

In general, the covariance term for any two firms, i and j, that have at least one market in common is given by $\alpha_{ij}\sigma_m^2$ where the coefficient α_{ij} equals the sum of the cross-products of the D_{ij}'s from the firms' common markets.

We are now in a position to sum up. Realizing that some firms are specialized and others diversified to varying degrees and that a sample of firms might include a varying number of firms in various industries, the composition of the omega matrix will depend on which firms are included in the sample. If, for any sample, we factor σ_u^2 out of the omega matrix, the diagonal elements will consist of Herfindahl measures of product diversification: that is, the relative shares of the company's total sales accounted for by various markets in which it operates are simply squared and summed. If the firm is completely specialized, the appropriate diagonal element will be 1. If the firm is diversified, the element is less than 1. Any off-diagonal element for two firms that share no market will be 0. Any off-diagonal element for two firms that share at least one market, the ith and jth firms, say, will be given by:

$$\alpha_{ij}\frac{\sigma_m^2}{\sigma_u^2} = \alpha_{ij}K \quad (2.15)$$

ESTIMATION PROCEDURES

Again summarizing our results using matrix notation, let H_i equal the Herfindahl measure of the ith firm's product diversification. Let G represent the $n \times 1$ vector of g_{id}'s which are associated with the n firms of a hypothetical sample. Then,

$$E(GG') = \sigma_u^2 \Omega_2$$

where,

$$\Omega_2 = \begin{bmatrix} H_1 & 0 & 0 & \alpha_{14}K & \cdots & \alpha_{1n}K \\ 0 & H_2 & \alpha_{23}K & 0 & & \\ 0 & \alpha_{32}K & H_3 & 0 & & \\ \alpha_{41}K & 0 & 0 & H_4 & & \\ \vdots & & & & & \\ \alpha_{n1}K & & & & & H_n \end{bmatrix}$$

Apparently, the first, fourth, and nth firms share a common market, as do the second and third. The off-diagonal terms may differ from those in the Specialized Firm Model, however, because of diversification and the resulting α_{ij}'s.

Model III: The Diversified Firm, a More General Formulation

The above analysis assumes that diversified firms are mere aggregates of independent specialized entities. While the resulting formulation may be a useful first approximation, it does seem untenable from one standpoint. In particular, the firm-related error components of the various divisions of a diversified firm were assumed to be statistically independent. Though many examples could be given, one will suffice to show why this assumption might lead to unsatisfactory results. The quality of top-level management might well have similar effects on the "profits" of all divisions of the diversified firm. The e_{ij}'s of the various divisions would then be related.

This possibility suggests still another manner in which the error component might be decomposed. The variables affecting division performance may be classified according to whether their effects are unique to (1) the division, (2) all divisions within a firm, or (3) all firms and/or divisions in a market. For the division of the ith diversified firm selling in market j:

$$R_{ij} = a + bM_j + hY_{ij} + wF_i + u_{ij} \qquad (2.16)$$

where:

R_{ij} = the ratio of economic profit to sales for the division of firm i which sells in market j.
M_j = a market-related variable which affects, in the same way, all specialized firms and/or divisions that operate in market j,
Y_{ij} = a division-related variable with an unique effect on the division of firm i operating in market j,
F_i = an organization-related variable which affects, in the same way, all divisions (there may be only one) of the ith firm.
u_{ij} = an error term resulting from the omission of independent variables.

On the rationale of omitted variables, the disturbance term is again decomposed:

$$u_{ij} = m_j + f_i + y_{ij} \qquad (2.17)$$

where m_j is again that portion of the total error term attributable to the omission of market-related variables and where f_i and y_{ij} result from the omission of organization and division-related variables, respectively. Again it is assumed that each component of the total error term has an expected value of zero and a finite variance and is normally distributed. By definition, m_j is constant across all divisions or firms in market j and f_i is constant across all divisions of firm i, so that $C(m_j y_{ij}) = C(f_i y_{ij}) = 0$, for any i or j. It will be assumed:

$E(m_j f_i)$ = 0, always
$E(m_k m_j)$ = 0, for $k \neq j$
$E(m_k y_{ij})$ = 0, for $k \neq j$
$E(y_{ij} y_{pk})$ = 0, for either $j \neq k$ or $p \neq i$
$E(y_{pk} f_i)$ = 0, for $p \neq i$
$E(f_p f_i)$ = 0, for $p \neq i$

Consider the ith diversified firm which operates two divisions, one in market j and the other in market k. For these two divisions, with sales of S_{ij} and S_{ik} and profits of P_{ij} and P_{ik}, the profit function can be expressed:

ESTIMATION PROCEDURES

$$R_{ij} = \frac{P_{ij}}{S_{ij}} = a + bM_j + cF_i + hY_{ij} + m_j + f_i + y_{ij} \tag{2.18}$$

$$R_{ik} = \frac{P_{ik}}{S_{ik}} = a + bM_k + cF_i + hY_{ik} + m_k + f_i + y_{ik} \tag{2.19}$$

so that:

$$P_{ij} = (a + bM_j + cF_i + hY_{ij} + m_j + f_i + y_{ij}) S_{ij} \tag{2.20}$$

and likewise for P_{ik}. For the aggregate profit rate for the ith diversified firm, R_{id} is given as:

$$R_{id} = \frac{P_{id}}{S_{id}} = \frac{P_{ij} + P_{ik}}{S_{ij} + S_{ik}}$$

$$= a(D_{ik} + D_{ij}) + b(D_{ij}M_j + D_{ik}M_k)$$

$$+ cF_i(D_{ij} + D_{ik}) + h(D_{ij}Y_{ij} + D_{ik}Y_{ik})$$

$$+ (D_{ij}m_j + D_{ik}m_k) + f_i(D_{ij} + D_{ik}) + (D_{ij}y_{ij} + D_{ik}y_{ik}) \tag{2.21}$$

Of course, D_{ij} and D_{ik} sum to 1, and Equation (2.21) may be rewritten thus:

$$R_{id} = a + b(D_{ij}M_j + D_{ik}M_k) + cF_i + h(D_{ij}Y_{ij} + D_{ik}Y_{ik})$$

$$+ (D_{ij}m_j + D_{ik}m_k) + f_i + (D_{ij}y_{ij} + D_{ik}y_{ik}) \tag{2.22}$$

Again, calling the composite error term of the ith diversified firm g_{id}, it can be shown that:

$$E(g_{id}) = 0 \tag{2.23}$$

$$V(g_{id}) = E(g_{id})^2 = \sigma_f^2 + (D_{ik}^2 + D_{ij}^2)(\sigma_m^2 + \sigma_y^2) \tag{2.24}$$

Where the pth diversified firm operates a division in market j, but none in k:

$$C(g_{id}g_{pd}) = (D_{ij} + D_{pj})\sigma_m^2 \tag{2.25}$$

In general where two firms operate in m markets:

$$V(g_{id}) = \sigma_f^2 + \sum_{j=1}^{m} D_{ij}^2 (\sigma_m^2 + \sigma_y^2) \qquad (2.26)$$

The covariance terms are the same as before. Where two firms have no markets in common, for example, covariance is zero. Otherwise:

$$C(g_{id} g_{pd}) = \alpha_{ip} \sigma_m^2 \qquad (2.27)$$

For the same sample of firms, the variance-covariance matrix for the error term in the General Model, $\sigma_u^2 \Omega_3$, differs from the corresponding matrix in the Diversified Firm Model, $\sigma_u^2 \Omega_2$, in the following respect: to each diagonal element of Ω_2 is added σ_f^2. (The off-diagonal elements are, as noted, identical.) It becomes apparent that the original system of heteroskedasticity is dampened by the addition of the homoskedastic term σ_f^2. This is not unexpected. The object of this model was to account for any interdependence which might exist between the error terms of the diversified firm's divisions. Moreover, as σ_f^2 becomes smaller relative to σ_m^2 and σ_y^2, the configuration of Ω_3 tends toward Ω_2. As σ_f^2 becomes larger relative to σ_m^2 and σ_y^2, the configuration of Ω_3 approaches the identity matrix.

One may correctly accept classical least squares as an appropriate means of estimating the parameters of Equation (2.1) in the hypothetical case of the single-product enterprise with a fortuitous sample of firms, one from each industry. If some sample firms are diversified and/or the sample contains more than one firm from any one industry, then it appears likely that generalized least squares is the appropriate estimation procedure. In this latter case, the classical least squares estimates of the regression coefficients are unbiased though they are not minimum variance (best) and the estimated standard errors of the coefficients are meaningless.[3]

A Note on Implementation

While Model III appears to be the most satisfactory formulation on theoretical grounds, at least in comparison with other formulations developed above, it also poses the most serious problems for actual implementation. Specifically the parameters of Ω_3 include three ratios, each consisting of a variance divided by the total variance. For the model to be operational, at least two of these ratios must be known or estimatable. They cannot be determined in advance, however, and accurate estimation would appear to be a hazardous and costly process.

The problems encountered in the application of Model II are less formidable. If a breakdown of company sales by industry were available for each firm in the sample, all elements of Ω_2 would be known except for one variance ratio, namely, the omega ratio or its complement. By definition such a ratio must lie between 0 and 1, and one could proceed with estimation at alternative values, checking the sensitivity of statistical results to changes in the ratio's magnitude. Use of Model II of course assumes that σ_f^2 equals zero, but two-way sensitivity analysis involving nonzero values of this parameter quickly gets out of hand from the computational standpoint. More importantly, analysis of *CLS* residuals might provide some evidence as to the validity of this expediting assumption. This briefly was the plan for the empirical work on structure-profit relationships reported on below. More specifically, we collected the necessary data in a field survey and computed all elements of the Ω_2 except the omega ratio, K. That ratio was set at three alternative levels within the acceptable range of 0 to 1. The omega matrix proved to be singular where the ratio was set equal to 1.0, and we chose the values 0.0, 0.5, and 0.8.[a]

Model II proved to be inappropriate for analysis of structure-progress relationships. Estimation of these equations involved using an ad hoc procedure based on Model III. The details are given in Chapter 6.

---

[a]In a sample with n firms and m markets, it can be shown that where $K = 1.0$, Ω_2 is equal to DD' where D is $n \times m$. Because Ω_2 is $n \times n$ it will be singular if $m < n$, a likely condition but one that is not necessary where firms are diversified.

3 Sample Selection and Survey Procedure

A major problem in the quantification of structure-performance relationships concerns the availability of data which allow relating, with tolerable accuracy, theoretical constructs to their empirical counterparts. Relating economic profit to accounting profit, delineating aggregates of firms and/or company divisions that are to be treated as industries, and finding measures of product differentiation are but a few important examples. If anything, the estimation procedures outlined above suggest that the gap between data needs and the availability of data from secondary sources is even larger than has been supposed.

In order to supplement secondary data sources, a field survey was deemed necessary. Survey firms were selected as follows: from the *Fortune Plant and Product Directory*,[1] all those firms engaged in SIC major group 20 or 21 were first identified. Those not primarily engaged in sector 20 or sector 21 were eliminated as were those with substantial nonfood operations that would have entailed costly data collection. The result was a listing of well over one hundred manufacturing firms qualified for the survey. These firms were contacted through a letter containing a brief description of the project and a request for a personal interview with "an employee knowledgeable of company-wide operations." Because much of the information sought was of a confidential nature, nondisclosure of company data was guaranteed. Follow-up phone calls were made to arrange interviews. The persons interviewed were invariably executive officers of the company but beyond that no generalizations can be made. As often as not, many departments were involved in the interview. In some instances, answers were supplied by mail subsequent to the interview. Over eighty companies were interviewed and of these, seventy-nine were eventually included in the sample.

Some companies indicated a willingness to cooperate in the project but were unable to grant interviews at the time requested. The geographic location of others would have made personal interviews prohibitively expensive. For these reasons, over thirty companies were surveyed by mail. The schedules were prepared individually for each company and were supplemented where necessary with phone calls. The information gathered in this manner brought the sample size to ninety-nine firms. Their names are given in Table 3-1.

The sample of firms is obviously not a random one. There is a bias toward large firms and toward industries where the average firm size is large. Table 3-2 shows the number of firms primarily engaged in each of several broadly defined product groups. For 1963, the average sales of sample firms was $305 million,

Table 3-1
Sample of Companies

Allied Mills
Amalgamated Sugar
American Bakeries
American Crystal Sugar
American Maize
American Sugar
American Tobacco
Anheuser-Busch
Armour
Bayuk Cigars
Beam
Beatrice Foods
Beech-Nut
Booth Fisheries
Brach
Brown-Forman
Burrus Mills
Campbell Soup
Campbell-Taggart
Canada Dry
Carnation
Centennial Flour Milling
Central Soya
Coca-Cola
Colorado Milling & Elevator
Consolidated Cigars
Continental Baking
Corn Products
Cudahy Packing
Dean Foods
Del Monte
Dreweries
Duffy-Mott
Duquesne Brewing
Fairmont Foods
Falstaff Brewing
Foremost Dairies
General Foods
General Host
General Mills
Gerbers
Great Western Sugar
Green Giant
Heinz
Hershey
Heublein
Holly Sugar
Hormel
Hunt Foods
Hygrade

International Flavor & Fragrance
Interstate Bakeries
Kahn's
Keebler
Kellogg
Langendorf
Libby-McNeill
Liggett & Myers
Lorillard (P.)
Mayer (Oscar)
McCormick
Morrell
National Biscuit
National Starch & Chemical
National Sugar Refining
Nebraska Consolidated Mills
Needham Packing
North American Sugar
Olympia Brewing
Pabst
Penick & Ford
Pepsi Cola
Pet Foods
Peter Paul
Philip Morris
Pillsbury
Producer's Cotton Oil
Publicker
Quaker Oats
Ralston-Purina
Rath Packing
Savannah Sugar Refining
Schenley's
Schlitz
Schluderberg-Kurdle
Seaboard Allied Milling
Seagrams
Seeman Bros.
Staley
Standard Brands
Stokeley Van Camp
Sucrest
Sunshine
Tobin Packing
Utah-Idaho Sugar
Van Camp Seafood
Ward Foods
Wilson
Wrigley

Table 3-2
Number of Sample Companies Classified According to Primary Sector

Primary Sector[a]	Number of Firms
Fresh and processed meat	11
Beet and cane sugar refining	10
Flours and flour-related products	7
Soft-baked goods	7
Brewing products	6
Distilling and bottling	6
Preserved fruits and vegetables	6
Cigarettes	4
Chocolate and candy	4
Fresh dairy products	4
Grocery items	4
Oil seed products	4
Wet corn milling products	4
Hard-baked goods	3
Soft drink sirups and bottled soft drinks	3
Canned specialties	2
Cereal products	2
Cigars	2
Fresh, frozen, and canned fish	2
Manufactured dairy products	2
Prepared animal feeds	2
Others	4
Total	99

[a] In total, the firms are engaged in 45 different food, beverage, and tobacco manufacturing industries.

ranging from $18 million to almost $2 billion. Their combined 1963 sales of products classified in SIC 20 and 21 were almost $30 billion and accounted for over 40% of the total value of shipments in those sectors for that year.

The object of the interviews and the mail survey was to obtain information concerning both the nature of the industries in which the firms operated and the operations of the firm itself. The industry information sought pertained to market definition, concentration, and minimum plant scale. At the outset of the field survey, questions pertaining to multi-plant economies and minimum competitive firm sizes were also asked. These questions were soon abandoned for reasons that will be noted presently.

With regard to company operations, the questions covered such areas as company sales breakdown into various product groups, market share data, the extent of foreign production, the extent of vertical integration, the classification of company sales into private-label and producer-good type markets, expenditures on mass media, and research and development activities. Greater detail on the nature of the interviews will be given in subsequent discussion of the data analyzed in this study.

The fact that our sample is not random detracts from the meaningfulness of our statistical results. In several respects, however, the selection of such a sample was critical to collection of the needed data. Of major importance is a new set of industry definitions developed for this study. The construction of concentration statistics for these industries called for information on sales breakdowns and/or market shares from the largest firms in each industry. In addition, the collection of data on individual company operations was greatly facilitated by the exclusion of small firms. More comprehensive financial data are available for large corporate firms. Estimates of mass media expenditures are available for large firms. A file of McGraw-Hill plant census data, provided by the Economic Research Service of the U.S. Department of Agriculture, gave four-digit employment data for large companies. Various other secondary sources too numerous to mention provide information concerning large firms in selected industries. These, as well as the specific sources mentioned above, served to supplement the information gathered in the survey and allowed cross-checking for accuracy.

4 Industry Definitions

We have previously defined a selling industry as a group of firm selling products that are viewed as close substitutes by a common group of buyers. Two products may be said to be close substitutes if the elasticity of the cross demand function, corrected for real income effects, is very high. Presumably, then, firms and divisions are not to be included in the same industry unless the products perform similar functions for buyers. Appropriate attention must also be given to spatial and temporal dispersions of buyers and sellers in light of transfer costs. No firm or division should be excluded if its product competes closely with products of firms and divisions that are included. Obviously, any one firm might belong to several industries.

One further aspect of industry definition merits brief comment here. Many researchers have argued that substitutability in production should be taken into account in defining industries.[1] We argue that this suggestion has little merit on purely theoretical grounds. Suppose that two products, A and B, can be produced with virtually the same productive capacity. It may, nonetheless, be true that A is a very poor substitute for B from the viewpoint of buyers. There may, moreover, be quite different barriers to entry as between A and B because of differing levels of product differentiation. Thus, it is quite possible that economic conditions in the production of B may have little or no influence on competition among producers of A.

This is not to say that there is no merit in combining three industries, say, where the structural dimensions of all three are very similar and where firms are all equally diversified among them. In this latter case, however, the justification for aggregation runs in terms of statistical implications rather than economic theory. In a similar vein, where the researcher employs a concentration ratio as a single measure of overall structure, there might be considerable merit in combining two industries where it is known that firms in one can easily enter the other. Thus, for research purposes and in light of data shortcomings, combining industries on the basis of production substitutability might well be the best alternative way of proceeding.

Defining an industry as a group of firms selling close substitutes immediately raises a question for empirical research. How close is close? Confronted with the vexing problems associated with using fuzzy economic criteria in defining industries, researchers to the man have placed heavy reliance on the definitions provided by the Bureau of the Census.

The Census, in its Standard Industrial Classification (SIC) system, divides manufacturing into 21 major groups bearing two-digit codes. Major groups are, in turn, divided into industry groups (three-digit codes), which are subdivided into almost 500 four-digit industries. These industries are aggregations of still more narrow categories. For various reasons not worth going into here, the various aggregates are formed using criteria that differ substantially from those that economists use in defining industries. More specifically, the Census gives substantial weight to similarity of process—that is, to technological factors—in grouping economic activities. The competitive nature of products and firms is, as Conklin and Goldstein point out, "only one characteristic of an industry; others are methods of manufacture, types of facilities, and other physical or technological factors."[2]

The criteria employed by the Census lead to some results that are alarming from the viewpoint of economic research. Critical evaluation can be found elsewhere; a few examples will suffice here. A notorious example is the splitting of the sugar-refining industry into two four-digit aggregates, cane sugar and beet sugar, because of dissimilarity in refining processes. Another example from the food sector is the soft-baked goods aggregates which include bakers in New York along with bakers in San Francisco even though transfer costs prohibit intercity shipments.

The fact that economic criteria for industry definition differ from those used by the Census does not mean that the Census aggregates are of no use whatever in defining industries. What it does mean is that the Census aggregates are suspect. As we have already noted, however, many researchers have used, we feel rather blithely, various Census aggregates (the four-digit industries mainly) with or without corrections for the more blatant errors. This raises the extremely important issue of the sensitivity of statistical results to the choice of industry definitions.

In light of these considerations and because little work has previously gone into the framing of industry definitions, apart from culling and minor alteration of Census groupings, a sensitivity analysis was made on the basis of three alternative sets of industry definitions within the food sector. One set is simply the often-used Census four-digit industries, except that cane and beet sugar have been combined into one industry, as have the three four-digit oil crushing groups. (See Appendix Table A-2 for a listing of the relevant Census four-digit industries.)

A second set, and the one receiving the most attention in subsequent analysis, represents a substantial effort to define industries within the food sector that satisfy as closely as possible the economic criteria noted above. Only limited weight was given to production substitutability. In establishing these theoretic industries it was necessary to rely heavily on information collected in the survey and from knowledgeable academic personnel and various secondary sources. No particular level of Census classification was adhered to as four-digit, five-digit and seven-digit groups were merged or split. Census data [3] were of considerable value in the computation of various statistics for the new theoretic groups, however, and they are referred to as the *reconstructed census industries*. Subjective judgments were rendered at nearly every stage of the exercise, though it should be emphasized that one cannot avoid making such judgments, implicitly at least, by simply using Census industries. A listing of the reconstructed census industries with more detail on their composition is given in Appendix Table A-1.

The third set of industries consists merely of four-digit and five-digit Census groups that were chosen to correspond as closely as possible to reconstructed census industries. The choice was often difficult but preference was generally shown for five-digit rather than four-digit groups. This set of industries represents an attempt to apply economic criteria without the aid of the primary data needed to reconstruct industry concentration ratios. These industries will be referred to as the Census four-five-digit; they are listed in Appendix Table A-3.

5 Structure-Profit Relationships

As previously noted, the main objective of the research reported here was to test some of the major hypotheses in the field of industrial organization using multiple regression in an analysis of data generated by the food-processing sector. In this chapter, attention will be focused on the estimation of structure-profit relationships. Considerable use will be made of Model II, in which the diversified firm is treated as a mere aggregate of independent divisions. Structure-progress relationships will be taken up thereafter in an exploratory application of the econometric formulation which assumes that the various divisions within the diversified firm are interdependent.

The Variables

Dependent and independent variables analyzed in this study of structure-profit relationships are described below. The theoretical bases for the inclusion of most variables are well developed in the literature and merit only brief attention here.

Profit Rates as the Dependent Variable

There is some controversy over which profit rate is the most appropriate for use as a dependent variable in analyses of this sort, but fairly good arguments can be adduced in support of any one of several of them.[1] In addition, the various profit rates tend to be correlated. As noted above, however, an endearing aspect of profit over sales is its internal consistency with allocating the activities of the diversified firms among markets on the basis of sales. For these reasons we would prefer not to become embroiled in a controversy over which profit rate generally is the most appropriate and choose, instead, to summarize the bulk of our results using profit over sales and showing, for comparison, some results using Stigler's total returns to total assets, and the most commonly used rate, profit over net worth, Specifically, the alternative dependent variables are:

R_i = total profits, after tax and after a deduction for implicit returns to equity capital (0.05 times year-end equity), divided by total sales, ith company, for the period 1959-1967,

R'_i = total profits (before taxes) plus interest paid, divided by total year-end assets, ith company, for the period 1959-1967,

R''_i = total profits (after taxes) divided by total year-end equities, ith company, for the period 1959-1967.

All financial data were taken from *Moody's Industrial Manual*. [2] Averages over time are employed to avoid strictly short-run phenomena such as the business cycle. For a few sample companies financial data were not available for the full nine-year period. In no case, however, does the weighted average include fewer than four years. In every case the firm-related independent variables are based on the years for which financial data are also available. Accounting profits have been corrected for the omission of implicit rates of return on equity; shortcomings due to price level changes, differing time patterns of asset acquisition, arbitrary methods of computing depreciation and other anomalies arising out of the curious ways of accountants are merely recognized.

For the diversified firm, each of the following independent variables, except company size and diversification, is weighted according to the scheme suggested above in our discussion of estimation procedures; division sales are used as weights. In this connection, foreign sales are ignored in computing weighted variables, the implicit assumption being that structures of foreign and domestic markets are similar. (No attempt was made to collect data on the structures of foreign markets.) Take, for example, a company with sales abroad equaling ten percent of total sales and with 50% of its sales in domestic market A, where the four-firm concentration ratio is 0.5, and with 40% of its sales in domestic market B, where concentration is 0.7. The weighted concentration ratio for this company would be roughly 0.6, or (0.5 × 0.5 plus 0.4 × 0.7, all divided by 0.9). A further complication arises out of the operations of vertically integrated firms producing intermediate goods that could have been, but were not, sold in vertically related markets. In these cases, information was obtained through the field survey on the "sales value" of products produced in the various vertically related markets and the firm then was treated much as any other diversified firm. Suppose that a company produces an intermediate product with sales value equal to X dollars. Total sales would be inflated by this amount, X dollars, and the profit rate and weighted independent variables would be computed as if the company actually sold the intermediate output in a separate market. Finally, some companies are diversified because, in part, they sell in geographically separated markets. This was true of companies producing dairy and/or soft-baked goods. A weighting procedure using employment rather than company sales was dictated by the nature of available data. Milk marketing areas as defined by the USDA in administering milk marketing orders are used as geographic industries for fresh dairy products. Fortunately, data on employment in dairy plants by company by marketing area are available as are data on total dairy employment by companies.[a] The assumption here was that the ratio of "dairy employment" in a local market to total dairy employment of the company equaled the ratio of dairy sales in the local market to total company dairy sales. The same procedure was applied to soft-baked goods where each state is viewed as a geographic industry and where again the relevant employment data are available.

Concentration

The argument for including some measure of industry concentration as an independent variable is well worn. The ability to see the rewards associated with collusion and the willingness to participate in and enforce collusive agreements would appear to increase as concentration increases; the expected sign of the parameter for concentration is positive.

Several measures of concentration were estimated in this study including one, two-, three-, four-, and eight-firm concentration ratios for the reconstructed census industry definitions. These ratios were compiled from information on market shares of sample firms and their competitors and from other sources such as the Federal Trade Commission reports, trade publications, corporate reports, knowledgeable industry and academic personnel, and the like. The reconstructed census industries along with the four-firm and eight-firm concentration ratios and other data are contained in Appendix Table A-1. Concentration ratios for the Census four-digit and four-five-digit industries come directly from the Census and are given in Appendix Tables A-2 and A-3, respectively, along with other relevant data.

Thirty of the fifty-four reconstructed industries may be identified to some fair extent with Census four- and five-digit groupings. Though the definitions are somewhat at variance, our estimates of the four-firm concentration ratios are still within five percentage points of the nearest Census grouping. The remaining 24 estimated ratios are of a rough-and-ready sort, though we have checked our sources of information for internal consistency wherever possible. It is well to remember that the accuracy of concentration ratios in industrial organization research reflects not only accurate sales data by company, but also the definition of the industry. While the Census sales data might be more accurate than those collected for this study, the increased accuracy will be of little consequence if the wrong industry definitions are employed. An interesting question pertains to

---

[a]Company sales by geographic region were not collected in the field survey. The employment data mentioned above were purchased by the USDA from McGraw-Hill and were made available to us for this study. These data listed location, four-digit Census classification, and number of production employees for each plant for firms selling in geographic markets.

the manner in which the weighted concentration ratios by company are affected by alternative industry definitions. In Appendix Table B-1 we have ranked companies according to their weighted concentration ratios defined on the basis of adjusted census industry definitions, showing for comparison the associated weighted concentration ratios for Census four-digit and Census four-five-digit industries.

It is recognized that a concentration ratio is nothing more than an arbitrary point on the cumulative curve. These ratios may be employed in the analysis in various ways, however, and there is always the question of which measure is the most meaningful. Some of the resulting issues will be taken up briefly at a later point. The bulk of our statistical results is summarized using the following variable:

M_{1j} = sales of product j by the four largest sellers of product j divided by total market sales of product j, 1963.

Product Differentiation

The products of firms held to be in the same industry might be close but not perfect substitutes. In this situation, a firm with a highly differentiated product might be insulated from competition on the part of established and potential sellers alike. Quantification has involved both measuring the strength of various sources of product differentiation and using proxies that indicate magnitude regardless of source.

Advertising. Professor Bain and others have emphasized the importance of advertising expenditures as a major source of product differentiation.[3] This would appear to be especially true of the food sector, where the other likely determinants of product differentiation—product durability and complexity, integration of retail dealer-service organizations by manufacturers, and conspicuous consumption—would appear to be generally unimportant. Interestingly, in his study of barriers to entry for twenty industries, Bain ranked five "food" industries according to the extent of product differentiation; advertising outlays appeared in every case to be the most significant variable used in ranking.[4]

In the absence of better measures of product differentiation, researchers have used the ratio of industry advertising expenditures to industry sales. The FTC study, for example, uses the above ratio for three-digit Census groups in its analysis of company profit rate variation. Our measure, given below, departs from others in that it includes only traceable mass media. In addition, the ratio is computed for the firm rather than its industry.

Y_{1i} = total advertising expenditures in traceable mass media (all TV, radio, magazine, newspaper, and billboards) for the ith company, divided by total company sales for the nine-year period, 1959–1967.

Estimates of expenditures on traceable mass media were compiled from several secondary sources [5] for the years 1956, 1960, and 1967. Outdoor advertising was not included for 1956 and 1960 nor was radio for 1956. (The relative magnitudes of these latter expenditures are very small.) The data are subject to several shortcomings, the most serious being that they often understate expenditures of small regional firms.[a] In the field survey an attempt was made to correct for this and other deficiencies as well as to ascertain the validity of linear extrapolation over the periods for which the secondary data had not been secured. The estimates were adjusted with aid from respondents. No attempts were made to collect data on nonmedia promotional activities.

Research and Development. To some extent, of course, product differentiation rests upon real product difference that may or may not be heavily advertised. Partly for this reason we have included as an independent variable the ratio of company research and development (R and D) expenditures to sales.

Y_{2i} = total research and development expenditures divided by total company sales, ith company, for the nine-year period, 1959–1967.

Estimates of R and D expenditures by company were collected in the field survey. In interviews and in correspondence, R and D expenditures were defined as those "incurred to create new products and processes or improve old ones." An effort was made to use terminology close to that used by the National Science Foundation in their industrial surveys.[6] As a check on accuracy, the coeffi-

---

[a]Treating advertising and R and D expenditures (see below) as expenses rather than capital investments may lead to differences between true and measured profit rates. If current advertising outlay, for example, is less than current depreciation of advertising capital, the true profit rate on sales will be less than the measured rate; contrariwise if current outlays exceed current depreciation. Examination of the data suggest that most sample companies with sizable rates of advertising and R and D expenditures have been increasing those rates over the time period in queston. This does not mean necessarily that advertising and R and D capital has been increasing because such expenditures on the part of competing firms might well tend to be self-canceling. Moreover, to the extent advertising and R and D capital is increasing, biases against our economic hypotheses are introduced. For these reasons, the possible differences between true and measured profit rates attributable to the "expensing" of intangibles are treated as the result of errors due to the omission of relevant variables. An analysis by Weiss suggests that the whole problem could easily be exaggerated. See Leonard W. Weiss, "Advertising, Profits, and Corporate Taxes," *Review of Economics and Statistics,* 51 (November 1969), pp. 421–430.

cient or correlation between R and D and number of patents secured (1959-1967), both expressed as a percentage of sales, was 0.94.[7]

Likely payoffs from research and development (R and D) programs are product superiority that might be hard to duplicate or a continuing stream of new product differences that keeps imitators at bay.[a] Other benefits flowing from R and D programs are the process advantages which allow the firm to produce at a lower cost than established or potential rivals. We do not contend that R and D programs are the only source of such product and process advantages but that they do indicate a conscious effort and perhaps the only consistently identifiable source. While product differentiation and process advantages may be overcome in the long run, the capital requirements associated with initial losses could provide a barrier to entry. There may also be scale economies associated with R and D and advertising programs which effectively impede entry.

Producer-Consumer Binary. An alternative to the measurement of particular sources or symptoms of product differentiation at the firm level is provided by a simple binary classification. Specifically, all markets or sectors of markets are classified as being either differentiated or nondifferentiated. The binary variable is assigned a value of 1 if the firm is in a market or market sector classified as differentiated. If the market or sector is nondifferentiated, a value of 0 is assigned. Such a qualitative variable obviously does not measure the degree of product differentiation but it does offer an alternative advantage. Presumably it registers the existence of differentiation regardless of source and is not dependent upon any relationship between the strength of consumer preferences and the level of some particular variable such as advertising.

Any distinction between differentiated and nondifferentiated goods involves a judgment on the part of the researcher. In this regard, however, the consumer-good–producer-good dichotomy has long been recognized as a fair device in attempting to measure the impact of differentiation. Though this scheme of classification was generally adhered to here, some of the specifics of application are worth nothing. All consumer goods sold under the brand name of the processor are treated as differentiated goods. Fresh meat is classified as undifferentiated because of the long history of unsuccessful attempts to exploit a processor's label in selling fresh meat. Of course, some industrues, such as flour and sugar, sell consumer goods as well as producer goods. In these cases all

---

[a]Our treatment of research and development activities as a source of product differentiation is not new. Williamson, for one, has noted that in the long run, research and development expenditures as well as selling costs are relevant in the determination of product differentiation barriers. See Oliver E. Williamson, "Selling Costs as a Barrier to Entry," *Quarterly Journal of Economics,* 77 (February 1963), p. 113. It should also be noted that advertising and R and D expenditures are firm-related variables. They should, theoretically, be collected on a divisional basis (for the diversified firm) and then aggregated by weighting. A moment's reflection will show, however, that this recommended procedure results in the same ratios as described above, which are then implicitly "weighted divisional variables."

producer-good sales are classified as undifferentiated. Finally, all sales destined for private labeling by the buyer were classified as undifferentiated.

The variable computed for the individual firm may be, and usually is, a weighted binary variable which corresponds to that firm's ratio of differentiated to undifferentiated sales. More specifically,

Y'_{1i} = total sales classified as differentiated for the ith firm, divided by the total sales of the ith firm, for the time period 1959–1963.

Not unlike Y_{1i} and Y_{2i}, the variable Y'_{1i} computed overall for the firm is consistent with the weighting scheme suggested earlier. That is, assigning a binary variable of 1 to a division if it is in a differentiated market, and 0 otherwise, and taking a sales weighted average over all divisions will result in the same value.

Relative Firm Size

The Federal Trade Commission has argued that the firm's relative market share, computed by dividing its market share by the share of the four leading firms in the market, measures the extent to which its product is differentiated. They state that "in consumer product markets characterized by non-price competition the market share that a firm possesses compared to the market share of the leading firms in the market largely reflects the extent to which the firm has been successful over the years in building up consumer loyalty for its products and brands and hence achieving a product differentiation advantage vis-a-vis its major actual or potential competitors."[8]

In our view, the variable is more correctly called a relative size variable. Mathematically, it is simply a measure of the firm's size relative to the average size of the four largest firms in the industry. This does not negate the FTC argument quoted above but reinforces their supplemental conjecture that relative size would reflect any size economies that may exist. Other factors might also be involved. A firm that has a history of superior management or progressiveness would likely be large relative to others. In fact, it appears to us that relative firm size is a proxy for a number of variables that might tend to enhance firm profitability.

The significance of this variable in the FTC study was encouraging and the variable has been computed, using survey data, for our sample of firms for both reconstructed and four-digit Census definitions.

Y_{3i} = sales of product j by the ith company divided by the sales of product j by the four largest sellers of product j, 1963.

Scale Barriers

Entry into an industry is impeded if optimum firm size is large relative to the industry and if diseconomies of a less than optimum size operation are large. In this case, the potential entrant must either depress the market price upon entry with an efficient-sized unit or operate at a size that is seriously inefficient. As Modigliani has shown, the actual magnitude of such scale barriers depends not only on the shape of the long-run average cost curve but on the elasticity of market demand as well.[9]

Available data have forced us to use estimates of minimum-optimum plant size which are based on the survivor technique applied to Census four-digit plant size data. Justification for this approach is that plant size alone may, to some extent, be important as a barrier. The variable is defined as:

M_{2j} = estimated sales of the efficient size plant divided by total industry sales, jth industry, 1963.[10]

That this variable is based on four-digit definitions is, of course, a shortcoming. It is also realized that economies (diseconomies) associated with firm size and differences in price elasticities of demand might render the estimates meaningless.

Firm Size

Baumol argues that size of the firm alone may contribute to a higher rate of return as a result of imperfections in the capital market. He states that "at least up to a point, increased money capital will not only increase total profits of a firm, but because it puts firms on a higher echelon of imperfectly competing capital groups, it may very well also increase its earnings per dollar of investment even in the long run after all appropriate capital movements are complete."[11] To test this hypothesis, two alternative measures of size are included in our list of variables. The first implicitly tests for a simple linear relationship between firm size and profitability.

F_{1i} = average of year-end total assets, ith firm, 1959-1967.

The second measure was first used by Hall and Weiss and later by the Federal Trade Commission.[12]

F'_{1i} = reciprocal of the log of average year-end total assets, ith firm, 1959-1967.

Growth in Demand

The growth of market demand has been cited both as an element of market structure and as a part of basic economic data.[13] The corresponding implications for its influence on performance may be quite different. Some of those who view growth as an element of structure (influencing performance via competitive behavior) hypothesize a negative relationship with profit on the premise that collusive agreements are more likely reached and made effective in cases of declining or slowly growing demand. Those who view growth as a part of basic economic data (operating directly on performance, independently of competitiveness) hypothesize a positive relationship, presumably because of a lag in supply response. As regards this argument, however, Stigler has noted that only those increases in demand that are not fully anticipated will support excessive rates of return.[14] Collins and Preston, noting the potentially conflicting theories of the impacts of demand growth on rates of return, refused to take a position on a priori grounds alone.[15]

Precise measures of demand growth over time are rarely available, and various measures of growth in output over time have been used as proxies in empirical research. We employ such proxies here, recognizing that the theoretical case for expecting either a positive or a negative sign is in shambles and that the alternative variables actually used to measure demand growth are, at best, very crude. The measure employed in this connection is:

M_{3j} = the compound growth rate for market j, interpolated from total growth index for market j, 1954–1963 for reconstructed census industries and 1958–1963 for Census four-digit and four-five-digit industries.

Conglomeration (Diversification)

Perhaps the most widely quoted writer on the subject of conglomerate bigness is Corwin D. Edwards, who views the big conglomerate firm with considerable misgiving.[16] Basic to his position is the belief that the conglomerate has substantial power because of the extent of its resources and its operations across many markets. It is unnecessary that the conglomerate have a substantial share of the business in any one market, though many conglomerates are so endowed. The aggregation of wealth plus diversification is all that is required. It is not our intent here to critically evaluate the arguments adduced by Edwards in support of his thesis; such evaluations are available elsewhere.[17] Rather, it is our intent to test the hypothesis that conglomerate bigness leads to excess profits. The following alternative independent variables were employed in this connection:

F_{2i} = the number of reconstructed census industries in which the ith firm is engaged, averaged 1959-1967.

F'_{2i} = the percentage of sales by the ith firm not classified in its primary reconstructed census industry, averaged 1959-1967.

F''_{2i} = the percentage of sales by the ith firm not classified in its primary four-digit Census industry, averaged 1959-1967.

F'''_{2i} = the percentage of sales by the ith firm not classified in its primary three-digit Census group, averaged 1959-1967.

Empirical Results

In turning to empirical results, it should perhaps be recalled that in the case of the Diversified Firm Model one component of the variance-covariance matrix of the error term—namely, the ratio of the variance of market-related error to the variance of total error—is not known and appears to be beyond estimation. This ratio, the omega ratio, must be assigned a specific numerical value if generalized least squares (*GLS*) estimation is to go forward. In the spirit of sensitivity analysis, the omega ratio alternatively is set equal to 0.0, 0.5, and 0.8. Estimates obtained from classical least squares (*CLS*) are also shown for purposes of comparison.

Major Overall Results

The estimated equations shown in Table 5-1 incorporate the independent variables used to measure concentration and product differentiation. Turning first to the reconstructed census definitions, the coefficients are all positive and in agreement with a priori expectations. The estimates are all unbiased in the absence of well-known specification errors but vary markedly from one formulation to the next. The estimates of the coefficient for the concentration variable (M_{1j}) increase as the omega ratio is scaled upward, whereas the estimates for the other two variables, advertising (Y_{1i}) and R and D expenditures (Y_{2i}) fall. We submit that the researcher using *CLS* estimation, unaware of the limitations noted above, would be immensely gratified by the t-ratios, which uniformly exceed 3. Yet these ratios lack meaning and the t-ratios in the *GLS* formulations tend to fall as the value of the omega ratio is increased. Importantly, however, the t-ratios are generally robust and, we feel, offer good evidence that the relevant population parameters are in fact positive. The evidence is especially compelling for concentration.

It would appear somewhat fruitless to devote much time to the consideration of specific values of the estimated coefficients in light of their variability over the various formulations. It should be borne in mind, however, that because payments to owner's equity capital have been extracted from net profits, the rate of return on sales is relatively low, averaging about 2.5% in our sample. In addition, the coefficients for advertising and R and D should in no case be interpreted in a normative manner. That is to say, one should not conclude that larger advertising or R and D programs will lead to greater firm profits regardless of the industry involved or previous levels of expenditure. Though these two variables are computed from firm data, they should not be interpreted strictly as being firm related. The role of total market expenditures on product differentiation, say, was noted, and ideally one might well include as one explanatory variable the market rate of expenditure and as another the firm's deviation from the market value. In summary, variables Y_{1i} and Y_{2i} are assumed to signal the existence of product differentiation that is identifiable with both the industry and the company's position within its industry. Implicit in the interpretation of the positive coefficients is the belief that these opportunities existed.

The producer-consumer binary, Y'_{1i}, was suggested as a proxy for *all* types of product promotion which accompany firm-originating brand names. For the equations of Table 5-1, the advertising variable was replaced by Y'_{1i} and the equations were reestimated. Using *CLS*, the sign for Y'_{1i} was positive and the t-ratio was 1.68. Using *GLS*, the sign remained positive but both the magnitude of the coefficient and the t-ratio declined rapidly as the omega ratio was scaled upward. When both Y_{1i} and Y'_{1i} were included in the formulations, the apparent significance of Y'_{1i} was very low with the sign switching in one case. The estimates for advertising were only slightly affected. These results did not support the hypothesis that there are any effects of product differentiation in addition to those attributable to advertising that may be isolated by simply using the consumer-good–producer-good industry dichotomy.

Regarding sensitivity of results to industry definition, the estimated coefficient and t-ratio for the one market-related variable, concentration, tend generally to be lower the greater are the departures of industry definitions from those judged to fit most closely economic criteria—viz., the reconstructed census definitions. The pattern is expected in that market variables would likely contain larger errors the less "theoretically accurate" the industry definition. The estimated coefficients and t-ratios for the quasi-firm variables, advertising and R and D, are generally greater the further are the departures of the industry definitions from the reconstructed census definitions. This pattern is not unexpected. The values of these two variables are not affected by the change in industry definition but their correlation with concentration is less the poorer the industry definition. Finally, the patterns of change in the estimates and t-ratios as the omega ratio is scaled upward seem to be about the same for all three sets of industry definitions.

As noted earlier, reconstruction of the Census industries involved mainly

Table 5-1
Ninety-nine Food Sector Companies: Estimated Regression Equations Relating Profit over Sales (R_i) to Three Explanatory Variables Using Classical Least Squares (CLS) and Using Generalized Least Squares (GLS) with Three Alternative Specifications of the Variance-Covariance Matrix of the Error Term

		Regression Coefficients with t-ratios in Parentheses			
Estimation Procedure[a]	Intercept	Four-Firm Concentration Ratio ($M_{1j'}$)	Advertising over Sales ($Y_{1i'}$)	Research and Development Expenditures over Sales (Y_{2i})	Coefficient of Multiple Determination (R^2)
		Reconstructed Census Industries			
CLS	−0.0084	0.0376 (3.44)	0.1977 (3.34)	0.6706 (3.72)	.459
GLS: 0.0	−0.0111	0.0393 (3.48)	0.2000 (3.31)	0.6751 (3.30)	.695
GLS: 0.5	−0.0164	0.0533 (3.01)	0.1433 (1.86)	0.5511 (2.14)	.428
GLS: 0.8	−0.0280	0.0747 (3.10)	0.1119 (1.29)	0.3761 (1.20)	.250

		Four-Five-Digit Industries		
CLS	−0.0019	0.0256 (2.49)	0.2541 (4.59)	0.8323 (4.81)	.429
GLS: 0.0	−0.0036	0.0222 (2.34)	0.2488 (4.17)	0.7712 (3.71)	.674
GLS: 0.5	−0.0030	0.0311 (2.07)	0.1830 (2.38)	0.7191 (2.85)	.400
GLS: 0.8	−0.0064	0.0394 (1.83)	0.1407 (1.67)	0.6117 (1.99)	.202
		Four-Digit Industries		
CLS	−0.0008	0.0189 (1.77)	0.2760 (5.02)	0.9000 (5.22)	.411
GLS: 0.0	−0.0015	0.0218 (2.04)	0.2643 (4.53)	0.8407 (4.13)	.670
GLS: 0.5	−0.0026	0.0327 (1.96)	0.1948 (2.58)	0.7643 (3.05)	.399
GLS: 0.8	−0.0062	0.0420 (1.73)	0.1528 (1.73)	0.6573 (2.15)	.199

[a]For GLS estimation, the omega ratio equals the value indicated. See text for interpretation.

identifying regional as opposed to national markets and placing a heavier reliance on the criterion of consumer substitution. The concentration ratios of the industries originally identified as regional—soft-baked goods and fresh dairy— were recalculated on a national basis and the equations given in Table 5-1 were reestimated. The new estimates, shown in Table 5-2, serve a dual purpose. First, for the reconstructed census industries, they yield some evidence as to the sensitivity of results to the inclusion of rather subjectively defined regional markets. Second, the procedure establishes exact geographic conformity between reconstructed census markets and those of the Census four- and four-five-digit industries. Any differences in results will therefore be due solely to variations in the *product* classifications of the alternative sets of definitions.

The manner in which the estimates are affected by the change in the geographic market boundaries for soft-baked goods and fresh dairy is not unexpected. The estimated coefficient for concentration and its t-ratio decline in any given formulation. The changes in the estimates for the other two variables are small and unsystematic. Despite these differences, it appears that failing to adopt the regional markets would not have altered the conclusions concerning the importance of market concentration in the reconstructed census industries.

One observation will suffice in comparing the estimates in Table 5-2 with those shown in Table 5-1 for the Census four- and four-five-digit definitions. The coefficients and t-ratios for the concentration variable are still stronger where the reconstructed census product categories are used, though the differences are not as marked in the absence of the regional market definitions. It would appear that at least some of the differences in the estimates for the reconstructed census market definitions as reported in Table 5-1, as compared to the Census four- and four-five-digit definitions, are due to differences in product classification alone. (We will hereafter retain our definitions of regional markets.)

At this point it seems appropriate to say something about the pattern of calculated residuals observed in the alternative formulations. Our analysis is based on reconstructed census definitions only. Under the assumptions set forth in the statistical model, the variance of the error term associated with diversified firms is directly proportional to the index of diversification, ΣD_{ij}^2. We would expect, therefore, that plots of the *CLS* calculated residuals would exhibit a wider scatter as this index of diversification rises. That is, of course, a case of heteroskedasticity. This pattern was in fact observed, especially when the two extremities of the range were compared. Equivalent plots of the calculated residuals from the *GLS* models do not display heteroskedasticity.

To analyze the residuals further, firms that have a similar predicted variance because of diversification (or size) are grouped together and the average squared residual is computed for each group. The average squared residual, though a biased estimate of actual variance for the group, may nevertheless provide an indication of the nature and extent of heteroskedasticity. Table 5-3 shows the magnitude of the average squared residual from the four quartiles of the sample

Table 5-2
Ninety-nine Food Sector Companies: Estimated Regression Equations Relating Profit over Sales (R_i) to Three Explanatory Variables Using Classical Least Squares (CLS) and Using Generalized Least Squares (GLS) with Three Alternative Specifications of the Variance-Covariance Matrix of the Error Term, Reconstructed Census Product Categories, National Market Areas

		Regression Coefficients with t-ratios in Parentheses			
Estimation Procedure[a]	Intercept	Four-Firm Concentration Ratio (M_{1i})	Advertising Expenditures over Sales (Y_{1i})	Research and Development Expenditures over Sales (Y_{2i})	Coefficient of Multiple Determination (R^2)
CLS	−0.0069	0.0373 (3.52)	0.1862 (3.07)	0.6508 (3.58)	.462
GLS: 0.0	−0.0049	0.0329 (3.18)	0.1781 (2.66)	0.6431 (3.03)	.689
GLS: 0.5	−0.0058	0.0383 (2.48)	0.1369 (1.66)	0.6035 (2.32)	.411
GLS: 0.8	−0.0093	0.0451 (2.09)	0.1106 (1.19)	0.5105 (1.62)	.211

[a] For GLS estimation the omega ratio equals the value indicated. See text for interpretation.

Table 5-3
Average Squared Residuals from Equations Estimated in Table 5-1 for the Reconstructed Census Industries by Quartile, Ordering Based on Characteristics of the Firm

Quartile	CLS		GLS: 0.0^a		GLS: 0.5^a		GLS: 0.8^a	
	Av. Sq. Residual	Percent of Q_4	Av. Sq. Residual	Percent of Q_4	Av. Sq. Residual	Percent of Q_4	Av. Sq. Residual	Percent of Q_4
			Ordered by D_{ij}^2, smallest to largest					
Q_1	0.00091	28	0.00480	106	0.00732	101	0.014183	83
Q_2	0.00183	58	0.00430	95	0.00727	100	0.014787	86
Q_3	0.00285	90	0.00340	74	0.00483	66	0.013580	79
Q_4	0.00315	100	0.00454	100	0.00728	100	0.017092	100
			Ordered by Sales, largest to smallest					
Q_1	0.00126	32	0.00520	113	0.01048	160	0.013284	75
Q_2	0.00139	35	0.00334	73	0.00488	75	0.013361	75
Q_3	0.00219	56	0.00391	85	0.00520	79	0.015287	86
Q_4	0.00390	100	0.00459	100	0.00654	100	0.017717	100

[a] The omega ratio equals the value indicated. See text for interpretation.

for each statistical formulation. The sample first was ordered by ΣD_{ij}^2, smallest to largest, and then by magnitude of sales, largest to smallest.

Note that the *CLS* residuals show a distinct pattern in both size and diversification orderings, though it is more distinct where the ordering is by extent of diversification. In this latter case, the average squared residuals tend to follow the predicted pattern, as the theoretical indices (ΣD_{ij}^2) for these quartiles are 0.18, 0.58, 0.93 and 1.00. Ordering by size seems to isolate higher variance firms in the fourth quartile, suggesting that our concept of diversification is not perfect. In this quartile analysis, as well as in the scatter diagrams, the *GLS* models generally appear to be free of heteroskedasticity.

In addition to the question of sensitivity of statistical results to industry definitions, there is also the question of which profit rate to use. Table 5-4 gives the estimated coefficients when total returns to capital and returns to net worth are used as alternative dependent variables. Only a sample of results is given to conserve space. (For more detail, see Tables B-2 and B-3 in Appendix B.) As noted previously, these measures of profit rates are not strictly consistent with the weighting scheme used in estimating the independent variables and in constructing the parameters of the hypothesized variance-covariance matrix. This may account for the generally smaller t-ratios relative to those obtained using profit over sales. It is also worth noting that the magnitudes of the estimated coefficients are consistent with the magnitudes of alternative dependent variables. More specifically, $R'_i > R''_i > R_i$, and for any independent variable in any given formulation, the estimated coefficient is higher the higher the dependent variable. Again the effect of using crude industry definitions is to lower the t-ratios for concentration and increase the t-ratios for advertising and R and D.

Numerous equations incorporating the measures of relative and/or absolute firm-size variables were estimated using both *CLS* and *GLS*. A cross section of representative results is given in Table 5-5. The coefficient of the relative-size variable has the expected sign and the t-ratio is quite substantial. This result is typical for all *CLS* and *GLS* formulations and for all industry definitions. Thus, the FTC hypothesis is given strong support. We continue to have some reservations, however, about the original economic rationale for including this variable in the first place.

Of the two alternative measures of absolute size, F_{1i}, the linear form, consistently provided the stronger estimates. When the only other independent variable is the four-firm concentration ratio, the coefficients of both size variables have the correct signs—assets with a fairly high t-ratio. Though this tends to support the Baumol hypothesis, the significance of the coefficients is substantially weaker with the addition of other independent variables. In fact, F'_{1i} has the wrong sign when relative firm size is included in the equation. The additional variables are positively correlated, to varying degrees, with either measure of size. In our judgment, the overall results for our sample lend support

Table 5-4

Ninety-nine Food Sector Companies: Estimated Regression Equations Relating Total Returns to Total Assets (R'_i) and Profit over Net Worth (R''_i) to Three Explanatory Variables Using Classical Least Squares (CLS) and Using Generalized Least Squares (GLS) with One Specification of the Variance-Covariance Matrix of the Error Term, Reconstructed Census Industries, and Census Four-Digit Industries

		Regression Coefficients with t-ratios in Parentheses			
Estimation Procedure[a]	Intercept	Four-Firm Concentration Ratio (M_{1j})	Advertising over Sales (Y_{1i})	Research and Development Expenditures over Sales (Y_{2i})	Coefficient of Multiple Determination (R^2)
		Reconstructed Census Industries: Total Returns to Total Assets			
CLS	0.0640	0.1047 (2.30)	0.6433 (2.62)	1.44 (1.93)	.277
GLS: 0.5	0.0050	0.2228 (2.76)	0.4280 (1.22)	1.18 (1.02)	.588

STRUCTURE-PROFIT RELATIONSHIPS

Reconstructed Census Industries: Profit over Net Worth				
CLS	0.0400	0.0865 (2.81)	0.4050 (2.43)	0.9284 (1.83)	.301
GLS: 0.5	0.0219	0.1114 (2.08)	0.4955 (2.13)	1.044 (1.34)	.621
Census Four-Digit Industries: Total Returns to Total Assets				
CLS	0.0837	0.0566 (1.31)	0.8527 (3.83)	2.0780 (2.98)	.250
GLS: 0.5	0.0613	0.1404 (1.85)	0.6374 (1.86)	2.0733 (1.83)	.570
Census Four-Digit Industries: Profit over Net Worth				
CLS	0.0627	0.0277 (0.93)	0.6166 (4.02)	1.4729 (3.06)	.249
GLS: 0.5	0.0530	0.0602 (1.20)	0.6144 (2.72)	1.4997 (2.00)	.608

[a]For GLS estimation, the omega ratio equals the value indicated. See text for interpretation.

Table 5-5
Ninety-nine Food Sector Companies: Estimated Regression Equations Relating Profit over Sales (R_i) to Various Explanatory Variables Using Generalized Least Squares (GLS) with Omega Ratio Equal to 0.5, Reconstructed Census Industries

Intercept	Regression Coefficients with t-ratios in Parentheses						Coefficient of Multiple Determination (R^2)
	Four-Firm Concentration Ratio (M_{1i})	Advertising over Sales (Y_{1i})	Research and Development Expenditures (Y_{2i})	Relative Firm Size (Y_{3i})	Assets (F_{1i})	Inverse of Log Assets (F'_{1i})	
0.0027	0.0706 (4.45)				0.0018 (1.85)		.405
-0.0171	0.0512 (2.89)	0.1106 (1.38)	0.5416 (2.11)		0.0014 (1.41)		.440
-0.0229	0.0508 (2.94)	0.0995 (1.27)	0.4876 (1.94)	0.0250 (2.33)	0.0005 (.50)		.471
-0.0226	0.0727 (4.54)					-0.2696 (1.27)	.394
0.0012	0.0516 (2.89)	0.1265 (1.59)	0.5472 (2.12)			-0.1928 (0.90)	.433
-0.0279	0.0518 (2.99)	0.1122 (1.45)	0.4851 (1.93)	0.0279 (2.54)		0.0492 (0.21)	.470

to the Baumol hypothesis in a limited context only. That is to say, when product differentiation and other factors that may be associated with firm size are taken into account, absolute firm size offers little additional explanatory power.

The formulations reported in Table 5-1 were modified by adding, one at a time, each of the following three independent variables: plant scale barrier to entry, M_{2j}; market growth, M_{3j}; and diversification, with four alternative measures employed. Regarding M_{2j}, the estimated coefficient was always positive, as expected, but the t-ratios were not very impressive using CLS estimation and were even lower in the various GLS formulations. Using reconstructed census industry definitions, for example, and setting the omega ratio equal to 0.5, the estimated coefficient equaled 0.3571 with a t-ratio equal to 1.07. (For more detail, see Tables B-4, B-5, and B-6 in Appendix B.) Interestingly, though we don't know quite what to make of it, the inclusion of M_{2j} plays havoc with the t-ratios for concentration when Census four-digit industries are used. Similar results have been reported by Comanor and Wilson,[18] who suggest that multicolinearity is partly to blame.

The estimated coefficients for M_{3j} were positive with small t-ratios using CLS and GLS with zero off-diagonal elements; the estimates for the initial three independent variables were not greatly affected. The estimated coefficients were negative with t-ratios in excess of 3.0, however, when GLS was used with non-zero off-diagonal elements. The results were obviously highly sensitive to the statistical procedure used and, on balance, offer little support for the hypothesis that market growth has a systematic effect on company profit rates.

Estimates did not support the hypothesis that the extent of diverisfication is positively related to profit rates. The estimated coefficients obtained by using one measure of diversification, F'''_{2i}, were consistently positive but without acceptable significance. The other three measures of diversification consistently produce coefficients with the wrong (negative) sign and with large t-ratios in the case of F''_{2i} and F'''_{2i}. These results were not altered by the inclusion of relative firm size, Y_{3i}, as an additional independent variable. It is recognized that out tests scarcely do justice to the literature of the conglomerate firm.

The Effects of Concentration Examined in More Detail

As we have seen, the four-firm concentration ratio is quite significant in all GLS formulations and for all rates of return, especially for the reconstructed census industries. As was noted earlier, however, this variable represents an arbitrary point on the cumulative absolute concentration curve. In addition, the cumulative concentration itself is but one dimension of the number and size distribution of firms. Other dimensions may also be important from the standpoint of competition and market performance. Still another matter of concern is the implicit assumption employed thus far that the relationship between the four-firm concentration ratio and division profits is linear and continuous. In light of the importance attached to concentration, it would appear worthwhile to explore some of these issues further.

The equations in Table 5-1 were reestimated for reconstructed census industries, using alternately the cumulative market share of the one, two, three, and eight largest firms in place of the four-firm concentration ratio. While the estimates for the two-, three-, four-, and eight-firm ratios did display systematic differences, a rationalization of those differences seemed at best difficult. Among the four ratios, it was impossible to determine which one produced in some sense the best results. Substituting the share of the largest firm for the four-firm ratio did, however, give rise to a noticeably weaker estimate in all formulations.

Regarding absolute concentration, Miller has shown how the nature of the cumulative concentration curve can be specified in more detail through using marginal concentration ratios. In an aggregative analysis he related rates of profit to: (1) the share of the four largest firms; (2) the share of the fifth through eighth largest firms; and (3) the share of the ninth through fiftieth firms. The second two variables are examples of marginal concentration ratios. In Miller's analysis the estimated coefficients of the first and third variables were positive while the estimate for the second was negative with a high t-ratio. It was argued that firms in the second relative-size category tend to act independently, as it may not be in their best interests to enter into collusive actions.[19] This independent action, of course, will have a negative influence on the rates of profit of firms in the industry. As the Federal Trade Commission has pointed out, the hypothesis has important policy implications.[20]

The several concentration ratios compiled for the reconstructed census industry definitions facilitated experimentation with alternative marginal ratios. Though the analysis is confined to the eight largest firms, the flexibility in dividing that group exceeds Miller's (Miller used Census data). In general, the results do not confirm Miller's observation that the share of second-echelon firms exerts a negative impact on the rates of profit in the industry. It is interesting to note, however, that the results most favorable to his hypothesis were obtained when the specific ratios used in his analysis—the four-firm absolute and the five to eight marginal—were employed. These two variables, in both the presence and absence of Y_{1i} and Y_{2i}, were analyzed with R_i and R_i'' on *all* three sets of industry definitions. Using *CLS*, the estimated coefficients for the marginal concentration ratios were consistently negative but the t-ratios were never substantial. In *GLS* models, the estimated coefficients had even lower t-ratios and, occasionally, a positive coefficient was observed. The effect on the estimates for the other variables included in the equations was negligible.

Implicit in the form of the weighted variables used in the above analysis is the assumption of a continuous linear relationship between the rate of profit and each of the causal variables. In the case of concentration, this assumption has been challenged by two alternatives. First, several researchers have suggested that the relationship is or might be curvilinear and some evidence has been marshaled to this effect. Second, others, including Bain, have argued that the relationship is discontinuous; that there exists a critical level of concentration such that industries with higher levels have uniformly higher profit rates than do industries with lower levels. In what follows, an analysis that considers both of these proposals is described. As concerns the diversified firm, however, caution must be exercised lest the weighting scheme nullify the validity of the statistical tests. An example will elucidate the important issues.

Suppose the following: It is desired to test the hypothesis that firms earn a higher rate of return in industries where the four-firm concentration ratio exceeds 50%, say, than they do in those markets where the ratio is less than 50%. Many of the firms in the sample are diversified and for each has been computed the weighted concentration index. Consider sample firms A and B which operate in both markets i and j, the two markets having concentration "ratios" of 65% and 35%, respectively. Firm A's sales are allocated 70% to market i and 30% to market j so that its weighted concentration ratio is 56%. Firm B's sales are allocated 30% to market i and 70% to market j; its weighted concentration ratio is 44%.

Classification of the two firms to groups with weighted concentration indices above and below 50% for tests concerning the differences in the mean rate of profit for each of these two concentration classes will result in the misclassification of at least two divisions. Included in the high concentration group are the profits and sales (assets or equity) of firm A's division in market j, which should be classified in the low concentration group. A similar error is committed regarding firm B; its profit and sales in market i are misclassified in the low concentration group. Generally, to the extent that any of the sample firms operate divisions in both concentration classes (above and below 50%) the use of weighted continuous variables for purposes of discrete classification biases the tests. The mean profit rate of the high concentration group will always be biased downward, and counterwise for the mean rate of the low concentration group. The observed profit differences between the two groups is obscured and the null hypothesis is artificially favored.

Statistical tests involving group means do not necessarily imply the hypothesis of a discontinuous function, of course. Suppose, however, that there is in fact a discrete step function relating profits to concentration with the break occurring at the 50% concentration level. Given enough mixed observations from diversified firms, this discrete population function might be totally obscured in weighted firm data. It would also appear that linearly weighted concentration ratios and profits of diversified firms could be deceptive with respect to the true functional form in the case of a continuous nonlinear relationship. Consider the averages of profit rates of diversified firms which have been grouped by the decile in which their weighted concentration index falls. The mean rate of profit for each decile might represent profits from markets throughout the entire concentration range, the only restriction being that the weighted concentration ratio of the firms in the group fall in the specified decile. The grouping of profits (or residuals from the regression line) for diversified firms on the basis of the value of their *weighted* structural variables may therefore reveal nothing at all about the form of the underlying population function. To summarize, it would appear that using linearly weighted variables in light of company diversification would tend to conceal any discontinuities in the real relationship on one hand, or perhaps obscure nonlinear forms on the other.

Problems associated with discrete classifications and inspections of group means for information on the population functional form arise from a common cause and can be dealt with in a single manner. A proposed solution involves using binary variables at the division level (market level in sector analysis), classifying the divisions to the appropriate groups and weighting the binary variables for diversified firms. The rationale for this procedure will be demonstrated mathematically. For purposes of generality the example is modified to include more than one binary variable.

Consider the hypothesis of an increasing step-functional relationship between market concentration and divisional rates of return for concentration percentage ranges of 0-39, 40-69, and 70-100. Three market-related binary variables could be specified to accommodate this particular discontinuous functional form. The variable Q_1 takes on a value of 1 if the market falls in the low concentration range of 0 to 39, and a value of 0 otherwise. The variables Q_2 and Q_3 are specified in a similar manner for markets in each of the two higher concentration ranges. In regression analysis one of these categories must be deleted, of course, and the coefficients of the remaining two will represent estimated mean class differences (relative to the omitted class mean) rather than absolute values. Dropping Q_1, then, we can write the profit equation for the ith diversified firm's division in market j as:

$$R_{ij} = a + bM_j + cF_i + hY_{ij} + q_2 Q_2 + q_3 Q_3 + u_{ij} \tag{5.1}$$

or

$$P_{ij} = (a + bM_j + cF_i + hY_{ij} + q_2 Q_2 + q_3 Q_3 + u_{ij}) S_{ij} \tag{5.2}$$

If firm i also operates one other division, say in market k, the equation for total firm profits may be written:

$$P_{ij} + P_{ik} = (a + bM_j + cF_i + hY_{ij} + q_2 Q_2 + q_3 Q_3 + u_{ij}) S_{ij}$$
$$+ (a + bM_k + cF_i + hY_{ik} + q_2 Q_2 + q_3 Q_3 + u_{ik}) S_{ik} \tag{5.3}$$

STRUCTURE-PROFIT RELATIONSHIPS

or

$$R_{id} = a + b(D_{ij}M_j + D_{ik}M_k) + cF_i + h(D_{ij}Y_{ij} + D_{ik}Y_{ik}) \quad (5.4)$$
$$+ q_2(D_{ij}Q_2 + D_{ik}Q_2) + q_3(D_{ij}Q_3 + D_{ik}Q_3) + D_{ij}u_{ij} + D_{ik}u_{ik}$$

Assume that the concentration ratio for market j is 60, and for market k is 80. Noting the values of Q_2 and Q_3 for these two markets and looking specifically at the terms involving the binary variables, it can be seen that:

$[D_{ij}Q_2 + D_{ik}Q_2] = D_{ij}$, or the percentage of the firm's sales falling into the intermediate concentration range, and (5.5)

$[D_{ij}Q_3 + D_{ik}Q_3] = D_{ik}$, or the percentage of the firm's sales falling into the higher concentration range. (5.6)

The continuous values that these binary variables may exhibit are simply a result of the algebraic manipulation that is necessary to test a market- or division-related hypothesis using data from diversified firms. The discrete step-function still applies to the divisional rates of return and the weighted dummies will relate total company profits directly to that step-function if it is in fact appropriate. The example should also make it clear why, as noted above, unweighted dummies classifying the multimarket observation on the basis of the value of the weighted variable are not correct.

In a similar vein nonlinear continuous functional forms may be tested with multimarket observations providing care is taken that such forms are applied to the conceptional unit of analysis. Suppose one hypothesizes a quadratic relationship between the rate of return and some market-related variable. For the division or specialized firm, then:

$$R_{ij} = a + bM_j + cM_j^2 + u_{ij} \quad (5.7)$$

For firm i which operates in market j and k,

$$R_{id} = a + b(D_{ij}M_j + D_{ik}M_k) + c(D_{ij}M_j^2 + D_{ik}M_k^2)$$
$$+ D_{ij}u_{ij} + D_{ik}u_{ik} \quad (5.8)$$

which shows that nonlinear forms may be implemented only if they are anticipated prior to weighting. In this case, for instance, the squared weighted variable $(D_{ij}M_j + D_{ik}M_k)^2$ is biased upward from the conceptually correct weighted squared variable $(D_{ij}M_j^2 + D_{ik}M_k^2)$. As the firm becomes more diversified, the bias from incorrect weighting becomes worse. Note also that proper application of discrete and curvilinear forms concerns variables implicitly weighted for the divisions, such as our advertising variable, as well as those variables that are explicitly weighted. In these cases, however, nonlinear forms may be beyond testing because the values of the unweighted division variables are not known.[a]

On the basis of the above arguments, then, the following procedure was implemented to secure information on the form of the concentration-rate of return relationship in our sample. Nine binary variables were specified to classify all divisions of all firms to one of nine reconstructed census concentration classes. These variables are:

$DV10$ = 1 if M_{1j} lies between 0 and 19, 0 otherwise;

$DV25$ = 1 if M_{1j} lies between 20 and 29, 0 otherwise;

$DV35$ = 1 if M_{1j} lies between 30 and 39, 0 otherwise;

and so on for each remaining decile so that $DV95$ represents divisions in markets where M_{1j} ranges from 90 to 99. When weighted for a diversified firm, the value of each of these dummies will equal the proportion of that firm's sales in that particular concentration class. The sum of all nine dummies must equal 1 for the firm.

In analysis $DV10$ was omitted to avoid singularity in the matrix of regressors, so that the coefficients of the remaining binaries represent estimated differences of mean group rates of return with respect to the omitted class. Only CLS regression is employed. Where the dependent variable is return on sales and Y_{1i} and Y_{2i} are also included as independent variables, the estimated equation is:

$$R_i = .0038 - .0020DV25 - .0002DV35 + .0060DV45 + .0080DV55$$
$$\quad\quad (.0087) \quad\quad (.0091) \quad\quad (.0094) \quad\quad (.0117)$$

$$+ .0169DV65 + .0103DV75 + .0195DV85 + .0293DV95 + .1767Y_{1i}$$
$$\quad (.0126) \quad\quad (.0128) \quad\quad (.0112) \quad\quad (.0125) \quad\quad (.0693)$$

$$+ .7351Y_{2i} \quad\quad R^2 = .48$$
$$\quad (.1960) \quad\quad\quad\quad\quad\quad\quad\quad\quad\quad\quad\quad\quad\quad\quad\quad (5.9)$$

---

[a]The discussion here may be a bit belabored but not without reason. Several researchers have ignored the points made above concerning multimarket observations and weighted variables, particularly with respect to tests on discrete classifications. See, for example, Comanor and Wilson, pp. 430-433; the Federal Trade Commission, p. 29; and Stigler, *Capital Rates of Return*, pp. 66-67.

Table 5-6
Classical Least Squares Regression Estimates of Rate of Profit on Sales (R_i) for Nine Reconstructed Census Concentration Classifications— Based on Weighted Binary Estimates of Equation (5.9) with Y_{1i} and Y_{2i} Held at Their Mean Sample Values

Concentration Class as Based upon M_{1j} Reconstructed Census	Estimated Average Profit over Sales (R_i)	Average Value of the Weighted Binary for the Concentration Class
0.00 to 0.19	0.012	0.04
0.20 to 0.29	0.010	0.22
0.30 to 0.39	0.012	0.17
0.40 to 0.49	0.018	0.21
0.50 to 0.59	0.020	0.13
0.60 to 0.69	0.029	0.04
0.70 to 0.79	0.022	0.04
0.80 to 0.89	0.031	0.07
0.90 to 0.99	0.041	0.06

If the included variables are uncorrelated with the disturbance terms, the CLS coefficients are unbiased, though not minimum variance. The standard errors given in parentheses below each coefficient are biased. The sign and magnitude of the estimate for any particular binary variable depend, of course, on whatever class is omitted. The overall pattern of class differences is not arbitrary. Standard t-tests (potential CLS biases aside) are of little interest in that they test only for the significance of the difference between the estimated mean profit rate for an included class and the class that has been omitted.[a]

Table 5-6 shows the estimated mean rate of profit for each concentration class as computed from the above equation, holding the variables Y_{1i} and Y_{2i} constant at their mean values. The sample means for each weighted dummy are also given. A generally continuous relationship is revealed, with the classes for which the sample mean is low deviating somewhat. The class estimates are plotted at the concentration class midpoint in Figure 5-1. Also shown in the figure, for purposes of comparison, is the net regression line for the linear CLS regression of R_i on the weighted concentration ratio, M_{1j}, in an otherwise identical equation (Table 5-1). For the plotting of this continuous function the values of Y_{1i} and Y_{2i} were again held at their mean values. (It should be emphasized that the linear function in Figure 5-1 is not a least squares fit for the individual points that are plotted in the diagram.) The points represent estimated mean rate of profits for divisions in each concentration class. The linear contin-

---

[a]This explains why the apparent significance generally increases in the higher concentration ranges—that is, those classes farthest from the omitted or base class.

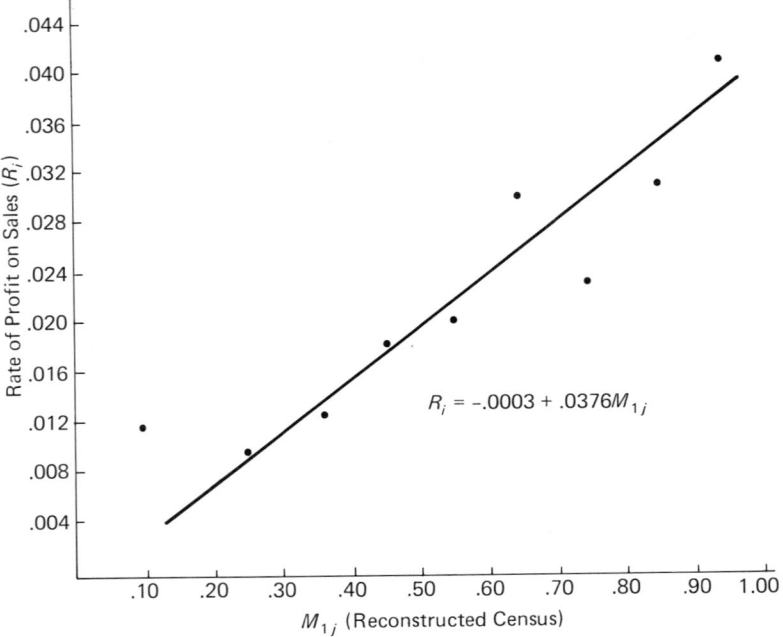

Figure 5-1. Alternative Classical Least Squares Estimates (CLS) of the Relationship Between Rate of Profit on Sales (R_i) and the Four-Firm Concentration Ratio (M_{1j}) for the Reconstructed Census Industries — Net Regressions for Linear (Table 5-1) and Weighted Binary (Equation 5-9) Variables.

uous function represents the "constrained" linear fit for average firm profits and a linearly weighted concentration ratio.

The estimates from the two regressions appear quite consistent, particularly in the mid-range where the sample means for the dummies are relatively high. The groups near the two ends of the range could have been aggregated into broader concentration classes to provide larger cell means. The object here, however, was to extend the range more fully to that observed for divisions and avoid as much averaging as possible. The class estimates at the upper end of the range where the sampling is lighter do not appear to deviate from the function in a systematic way. It would appear that the relationship between concentration and profits in this sample is approximately linear and continuous such that the linear weighted or "constrained" variable is appropriate. As one might expect, a quadratic form on concentration, computed for each division prior to weighting for the firm, yielded no additional explanatory power. The coefficient of the weighted squared term had an extremely low t-ratio.

6 Structure-Progress Relationships

As was stressed earlier, market performance is important because on the performance of the myriad markets that comprise the economy depends the extent to which human wants for material goods and services are satisfied. Not the least important dimension of performance is that of progressiveness in terms of the invention and adoption of new products and productive processes. A more neutral term for progressiveness is technological change. While excessive technological change appears to be quite possible, excessive progress smacks of incongruity. Whether too much or too little, however, it is clear that technological change has been a major contributor to our nation's economic growth. Based on the research of Solow and others, it seems quite certain that advances in knowledge far surpass the accumulation of physical capital in explaining increases in output per worker.[1] Small wonder, then, that economists are becoming increasingly concerned about technological change and its causes.

Following our previous schema, the determinants of technological change may be usefully grouped according to whether they reflect firm management, basic economic data, or market structure. While attention is focused here mainly on market structure, it is by no means certain that structure is the most important category of determinants. Management may be more or less disposed toward investing in technological change. Hohenberg has concluded, for example, that entrepreneurial proclivities were more important than market structure, raw material availability, and scientific opportunity in explaining the differences in progressiveness among French, British, German, and Swiss chemical industries from 1850 to 1914.[2] In terms of basic economic data, Scherer and others have adduced solid evidence in support of the contention that technological opportunities vary widely among different industries.[3] Obviously, we could expect greater investment in technological change and a correspondingly greater amount of change where the opportunities are pervasive and exciting. Markham also has called our attention to the extremely important fact that "in 1930 the outlays of private firms on research and development amounted to 0.1 percent of G.N.P. and in 1963 to 1.0 percent of G.N.P., a relative increase of 1,000 percent."[4] In light of the stability of market structure over time, it seems quite clear that variables other than structure—levels of educational attainment—are of utmost importance in explaining technological change.

Easily the most famous hypothesis regarding the association between structure and progress (or technological change) is attributable to Schumpeter, who wrote: "As soon as we go into details and inquire into the individual items in which progress was most conspicuous, the trail leads not to the doors of those firms that work under conditions of comparatively free competition but precisely to the doors of the large concerns...."[5] There is some agreement that Schumpeter had the *relatively* large firm in mind—the firm with market power—rather than one that is large absolutely. It is argued that the firm with monopoly power will have accrued the necessary financial wherewithal to carry on needed research programs. Its freedom from the rigors of competition allows it to devote time and money to innovation. Its large share of the market allows it to garner a commensurate share of the benefits from innovation; the benefits are internalized. As to incentive, Schumpeter argued that "a monopoly position is in general no cushion to sleep on. As it can be gained, so can it be retained only by alertness and energy."[6] Oligopolistic agreements to stifle competition would appear to be more difficult to reach and keep in the case of research and development than in the case of price.

At the theoretical level, Schumpeter's position has received both criticism and support. The result is a conceptual labyrinth, however, and one that we choose not to enter. Surveys are available elsewhere.[7] Our focus continues to be on empirical tests and, in addition to the hypothesis noted above—that monopoly power may be conducive to technological change—there are two additional neo-Schumpeterian hypotheses of interest.

The first asserts that large firms are more inclined and better able to bring about technological change than are small firms. The cost of innovation—if not of invention itself, then certainly its commercialization—is held to be so large that only large firms can undertake such a program. Innovation is risky; projects must be carried out in large numbers so that successes and failures can balance out. The small firm lacks resources and can ill afford to take the necessary risks. Finally, a percentage decrease in per unit costs resulting from a new process will lead to greater savings the greater the level of output; the large firm, therefore, has a greater incentive to invent new processes.

A second hypothesis, advanced by Richard R. Nelson, asserts that diversification is also conducive to technological change. He argues that research, particularly research of a basic nature, is a highly uncertain business and yields inventions in unexpected areas. A diversified firm is in a better position to recognize and commercialize a higher proportion of unanticipated inventions than is the highly specialized firm. Moreover, the increased breadth in the research and development program of the diversified firm offers increased insurance against a rash of unsuccessful research ventures. Nelson concludes:

> Yet it is the many-product giants, not the single-product giants, which have been most technologically dynamic, and, to the extent that we wish the private sector of the economy to support basic research, we must look to these firms.[8]

While the Schumpeter hypothesis and variants thereof have been the object of considerable empirical research, the tests used have been exceedingly simple and the results must be viewed as being quite inconclusive at the present time. The objective of the research reported here was to test the major hypotheses using techniques suggested by econometric models developed above and through estimating a more fully specified model than those estimated heretofore.

The Variables

In the statistical analyses reported on below, two alternative dependent variables were used to measure technological change. The first, Y_{2i}, was used previously as an independent variable in our analysis of structure-profit relationships. Defined here again for convenience, Y_{2i} measures technological change by the magnitude of research and development expenditures expressed as a percent of sales. The alternative, Y'_{2i}, reflects the level of inventive output that is patented. More specifically:

Y'_{2i} = number of patents issued to the ith company times 100, all divided by company sales, 1959-1967.[9]

Most of the major independent variables employed in the analysis of technological change have already been defined in the previous chapter on structure-profit relationships. In order to test the basic Schumpeter hypothesis, two variables, M_{1j}, the four-firm concentration ratio, and Y_{1i}, advertising expenditures divided by sales, are used here to measure the monopoly power of the firm. Absolute firm size, F_{1i}, is used to test the neo-Schumpeterian hypothesis that absolute bigness begets technological change. Diversification, F_{2i}, is used to test Nelson's hypothesis.

Although no account is taken of differing entrepreneurial attitudes toward investment in technological change, some effort is made to correct for differing technological opportunities available to the various firms. The food manufacturing sector has often been characterized as an old, mature sector with limited technological opportunities relative to such sectors as chemicals, electronics, and others. With the possible exception of corn products, we have not found much evidence of great variation in the opportunities from one food industry to another. Since some food companies have diversified into other than food industries, however, particularly into chemicals, it was deemed necessary to include a variable to account for the greater opportunities that are likely to be open to such companies. The variable used is given below:

Y_{4i} = total nonfood sales divided by total sales, ith firm, 1959-1967.

A moment's reflection will suggest that this variable is equivalent to a binary variable that takes on a value of 1 for each nonfood division and 0 for each food division, weighted by division sales for the firm as a whole. For this reason, this variable will be referred to as a nonfood binary.

Method of Analysis

In Model III, as set forth in Chapter 2, the variance of the composite error term, g_{id}, was shown to be equal to:

$$\sigma_f^2 + \Sigma D_{ij}^2 (\sigma_m^2 + \sigma_y^2).$$

The simple Diversified Firm Model, Model II, used in the above analysis of structure-profit relationships, assumes that σ_f^2 equals zero, that no organizational-related variable has been omitted (or exists). The assumption appeared to be a fairly good approximation on the basis of an examination of profit-rate residuals resulting from *CLS* estimation.

At an early stage of the analysis of progressiveness, the rate of R and D expenditures, Y_{2i}, was expressed as a linear function of several causal variables; the parameters were estimated using *CLS*. An examination of the residuals using scatter diagrams and quartile analysis similar to that reported on above revealed a result that was totally unexpected. The variance of the residuals was distinctly and systematically related to diversification as measured by our Herfindahl index, but the relationship was negative! Of course, it is always possible that we have unearthed nothing more than a statistical fluke. Still, an explanation would appear to be in order and all the more so if this phenomenon can be detected in other sets of data.

In the derivation of the econometric model it was assumed that the variance of each of the error components was constant. That the variance of the residuals from the estimated equations for progressiveness appears positively related to diversification suggests that such an assumption may be inappropriate in this particular application. The variance of the organizational-related component σ_f^2 is suspect. On a priori grounds, of course, there is no particular reason to assume that this term is small and nothing dictates that it be homoskedastic. The nature and proclivities of top-level management might be far more important in explaining R and D expenditure rates than in explaining profit rates. Note that if σ_f^2 is, in fact, relatively large and if its magnitude is related positively to diversification, then the magnitude of the total variance could increase with increases in σ_f^2 despite the discounting of $(\sigma_y^2 + \sigma_m^2)$ by the factor ΣD_{ij}^2. Because this after-the-fact observation has no particular theoretical merit, it is not presented here as an argument for the case at hand. The object is simply to point out that the observed pattern of heteroskedasticity is not necessarily inconsistent with the model.

Though the above explanation is at least plausible, the appropriate treatment is not very operational and the ad hoc treatment used here is not directly dependent upon it. The variance in the estimated *CLS* residuals appears most clearly related to the firm's number of reconstructed census industries, F_{2i}, and is roughly proportional to the three-fourths power of that variable. For this reason, $F_{2i}^{3/4}$ will be used as the diagonal term of the omega matrix. As noted, the observed pattern of heteroskedasticity says nothing about the problem of market-related autocorrelation and K will again be set at values of 0.0, 0.5, 0.8; that is, α_{ij} will be discounted exactly as in the profit analysis.

Two things should be noted concerning the consistency of this ad hoc procedure with the theoretical model and the tentative explanation provided above. First, on our explanation there should be simultaneous forces which operate to increase and decrease the variance of the total error term as diversification changes. The procedure adapted here accounts approximately for the net observable change only. Second, because the explanation consistent with the model dictates a relatively large value of σ_f^2, the relative value of σ_m^2 is necessarily restricted. High values of K are of course precluded in this case, and though $K = 0.8$ is included in the alternative formulations it is probably not as interesting as in the case of the profit equations.[a]

The Results

The estimated equations given in Table 6-1 contain variables inserted to test the three major hypotheses discussed earlier.[b] Turning first to reconstructed census industry definitions, the estimated coefficient for concentration has the expected sign, positive, and is robust across all formulations. The *t*-ratio falls only slightly as the omega ratio is scaled upward.

In an early stage of analysis, it became quite clear that the advertising variable was not lending support to the hypothesis that monopoly power as buttressed by advertising expenditures was conducive to R and D. The consumer-orientation variable, Y'_{1i}, on the other hand, always had a negative sign and very often had high *t*-ratios when *CLS* estimation was employed. This empirical regularity led to the belief that perhaps there was a tendency for firms selling undifferentiated products, especially producer goods, to have a higher propensity to invest in research than did the more consumer-goods-oriented companies. This

---

[a]It would be difficult to completely disregard autocorrelation, however, in light of Scherer's results concerning the differing technological opportunities among markets and the crude manner in which we account for such differences in our analysis.

[b]One firm was eliminated from our sample of 99 food-processing companies in the study of structure-progress relationships. This firm had both a very high R and D rate and a nonfood binary. Inclusion of the observation had an appreciable impact on the coefficient of the nonfood binary in some of the early estimation; it was therefore excluded.

Table 6-1
Ninety-eight Food Sector Companies: Estimated Regression Equations Relating R and Expenditures Divided by Sales (Y_{2i}) to Five Explanatory Variables Using Classical Least Squares (CLS) and Using Generalized Least Squares (GLS) with Three Alternative Specifications of the Variance-Covariance Matrix of the Error Term

		Regression Coefficients with t-ratios in Parentheses					
Estimation Procedure[a]	Intercept	Four-Firm Concentration Ratio (M_{1j})	Diversification (F_{2i})	Nonfood Binary (Y_{4i})	Firm Size (F_{1i})	Product Differentiation (Y_{1i})	Coefficient of Multiple Determination (R^2)
		Reconstructed Census Industries					
CLS	-0.0007	0.0110 (3.75)	0.0004 (3.29)	0.0360 (2.72)	-0.4626 (1.31)	-0.0040 (2.72)	.357
GLS: 0.0	-0.0004	0.0063 (2.88)	0.0004 (3.43)	0.0264 (2.26)	-0.4300 (1.51)	-0.0016 (1.53)	.490
GLS: 0.5	-0.0009	0.0062 (2.46)	0.0004 (3.44)	0.0247 (2.26)	-0.3639 (1.32)	-0.0010 (0.90)	.417
GLS: 0.8	-0.0015	0.0058 (2.18)	0.0005 (3.37)	0.0234 (2.17)	-0.2855 (1.09)	-0.0003 (0.22)	.380

			Census Four-Five-Digit Industries			
CLS	−0.0009	0.0103 (3.49)	0.0004 (3.42)	0.0336 (3.04)	−0.5717 (1.56)	−0.0027 (1.91)	.346
GLS: 0.0	−0.0010	0.0070 (3.17)	0.0005 (3.70)	0.0249 (2.15)	−0.5169 (1.79)	−0.0008 (0.81)	.499
GLS: 0.5	−0.0012	0.0067 (2.76)	0.0005 (3.60)	0.0235 (2.17)	−0.4182 (1.51)	−0.0003 (0.31)	.426
GLS: 0.8	−0.0017	0.0064 (2.47)	0.0005 (3.49)	0.0223 (2.09)	−0.3292 (1.24)	−0.0003 (0.28)	.388
			Census Four-Digit Industries			
CLS	0.0006	0.0063 (1.90)	0.0005 (3.31)	0.0336 (2.91)	−0.4172 (1.06)	−0.0027 (1.80)	.288
GLS: 0.0	0.0001	0.0041 (1.72)	0.0005 (3.66)	0.0249 (2.07)	−0.3927 (1.28)	−0.0008 (0.78)	.461
GLS: 0.5	−0.0000	0.0038 (1.51)	0.0005 (3.54)	0.0236 (2.11)	−0.3381 (1.17)	−0.0003 (0.30)	.394
GLS: 0.8	−0.0005	0.0037 (1.40)	0.0005 (3.45)	0.0223 (2.04)	−0.2725 (0.99)	0.0003 (0.25)	.361

[a]Using GLS, the omega ratio equals the value indicated. See text for interpretation.

hypothesis may or may not be supported by subsequent research but the *GLS* estimates shown in Table 6-1 are not very encouraging. The coefficient for the consumer goods orientation variable has a negative sign but the *t*-ratio falls off rapidly as the omega ratio is scaled upward. It is only strong where *CLS* estimation is used.

In summary then, the hypothesized positive relationship between market power and the rate of R and D expenditures is strongly supported by the results for concentration. A positive relationship between the rate of R and D expenditure and concentration has been reported by other researchers and, interestingly, Scherer has concluded that the evidence is especially compelling for techonologically sluggish industries. Our results are certainly consistent with his conclusions. The results for the consumer-goods orientation variable, on the other hand, suggest that product differentiation, in and of itself, does little to encourage technological change.

Nelson's hypothesis that company diversification fosters research is supported by our findings. The estimated coefficients for F_{2i} have the expected signs (positive), and the *t*-ratios are substantial for all formulations.

The hypothesis that asserts that bigness per se is conducive to research is not supported by our findings. The coefficient for the absolute-size variable has the wrong sign (negative) in some formulations and the right sign in others. The *t*-ratios tend to be rather low. Again our findings tend to be in accord with those of other researchers. According to Scherer, "a little bit of bigness—up to sales levels of roughly $75 million to $200 million in most industries—is good for invention and innovation. But beyond the threshold, further bigness adds little or nothing and it carries the danger of diminishing the effectiveness of inventive and innovative performance."[10] It must be remembered that our sample is composed of large firms; the average sales figure per company is roughly $300 million.

The estimated coefficients for the nonfood sales variable are positive and robust. This, of course, is not really very surprising in that its insertion in the equation grew out of observation of a rather low rate of R and D expenditures in the food sector relative to other sectors.

Turning to alternative industry definitions, the findings we have been discussing are, if anything, even stronger in the case of Census four-five-digit definitions. The coefficients for the concentration, diversification, and nonfood sales variable are remarkably stable whereas the *t*-ratios are generally higher in comparison to the results obtained using reconstructed census definitions. The results for the concentration variable are much less impressive, however, in the case of the Census four-digit definitions. Again we conclude that Census four-digit industry definitions are simply too crude for cross-section analysis of structure-performance relationships in the food sector. The generally unsatisfactory results for the absolute size and consumer-goods orientation variables using reconstructed census definitions are not appreciably better in comparison to the other two sets of industry definitions and merit no further comment.

The equations given in Table 6-1 were reestimated using rate of patenting, Y'_{2i}, as the dependent variable. Inspection of the resulting estimates and t-ratios, given in Table 6-2, shows a striking similarity to those given in Table 6-1. Since R and D expenditures are so highly correlated with patents issued, the similarities in findings should occasion little surprise. It might be noted, however, that the t-ratios for the estimates for diversification do fall substantially when patents issued is substituted for R and D expenditures as the dependent variable; the ratios for the nonfood to food sales variable are uniformly higher on the other hand.

Table 6-2
Ninety-eight Food Sector Companies: Estimated Regression Equations Relating Patents Divided by Sales (Y'_{2i}) to Five Explanatory Variables Using Classical Least Squares (CLS) and Using Generalized Least Squares (GLS) with Three Alternative Specifications of the Variance-Covariance Matrix of the Error Term

Estimation Procedure[a]	Intercept	Regression Coefficients with t-ratios in Parentheses					Coefficient of Multiple Determination (R^2)
		Four-Firm Concentration Ratio (M_{1j})	Diversification (F_{2i})	Nonfood Binary (Y_{4i})	Firm Size (F_{1i})	Product Differentiation (Y_{1i})	
		Reconstructed Census Industries					
CLS	-0.0004	0.0032 (3.24)	0.00007 (1.61)	0.0172 (4.73)	-0.2052 (1.75)	-0.0010 (2.10)	.344
GLS: 0.0	-0.0004	0.0017 (2.36)	0.00008 (1.92)	0.0132 (3.49)	-0.1518 (1.64)	-0.0001 (0.31)	.358
GLS: 0.5	-0.0004	0.0019 (2.35)	0.00008 (1.69)	0.0121 (3.42)	-0.1039 (1.16)	-0.0002 (0.71)	.312
GLS: 0.8	-0.0005	0.0018 (2.11)	0.00007 (1.54)	0.0114 (3.27)	-0.5905 (0.69)	0.0002 (0.42)	.281

			Census Four-Five-Digit Industries				
CLS	−0.0005	0.0032 (3.27)	0.00009 (2.04)	0.0165 (4.54)	−0.2458 (2.03)	−0.0007 (1.41)	.345
GLS: 0.0	−0.0005	0.0019 (2.66)	0.00010 (2.14)	0.0128 (3.41)	0.1776 (1.89)	−0.0001 (0.31)	.368
GLS: 0.5	−0.0005	0.0020 (2.59)	0.00008 (1.82)	0.0118 (3.33)	−0.1197 (1.32)	−0.00004 (0.13)	.321
GLS: 0.8	−0.0005	0.0020 (2.40)	0.00008 (1.64)	0.0110 (3.20)	−0.7193 (0.84)	0.00002 (0.05)	.291
			Census Four-Digit Industries				
CLS	−0.0001	0.0021 (1.96)	0.00010 (2.09)	0.0165 (4.37)	−0.2070 (1.61)	−0.0006 (1.34)	.298
GLS: 0.0	−0.0003	0.0013 (1.69)	0.00010 (2.21)	0.0127 (3.32)	−0.1529 (1.56)	−0.0001 (0.31)	.339
GLS: 0.5	−0.0002	0.0014 (1.70)	0.00009 (1.87)	0.0117 (3.26)	−0.1039 (1.15)	−0.00005 (0.14)	.293
GLS: 0.8	−0.0002	0.0013 (1.57)	0.00008 (1.69)	0.0110 (3.14)	−0.5922 (0.67)	0.00001 (0.02)	.266

[a]Using GLS, the omega ratio equals the value indicated. See text for interpretation.

7
Error Components in Aggregative Analyses

In the previous development and application of error component models, we have been mainly interested in the firm as a unit of inquiry. We now turn briefly to some of the main implications of these models for estimation of structure-performance relationships using industry and sector observations. The validity of our earlier assertion that the problem of heteroskedasticity might well arise in aggregative analyses will be established. We will have some comments on the observed propensity for higher levels of aggregation to give rise to stronger statistical results. As it turns out, our narrative will also shed further light on the usefulness of analyses based on company observations.

For the purpose of exposition, it will be assumed that in an analysis of profits, σ_f^2 is very small; that is, the special case of Model II in which the diversified firm is viewed as a mere aggregate of specialized divisions is approximately applicable. A few notes on the results for Model III will also be given, however.

Turning first to analysis using industry observations, the exposition proceeds as if one were estimating industry rates of return from a sample of specialized firms. The results are easily generalized to cover the alternative method of using Census plant data on value added. Consider, then, a profit function for the ith specialized firm in industry j:

$$R_{ij} = a + bM_j + u_{ij} \tag{7.1}$$

Firm-related variables are intentionally suppressed. Aggregating financial data for firm i plus a second specialized firm, say the hth, to estimate the industry rate of return and denoting the sales and economic profit for the aggregate as S_j and P_j, respectively, we have by definition:

$$S_j = S_{ij} + S_{hj} \tag{7.2}$$

$$P_j = P_{ij} + P_{hj} \tag{7.3}$$

The equation for the "industry" rate of profit can then be written as:

$$R_j = \frac{P_{ij} + P_{hj}}{S_{ij} + S_{hj}} = a + bM_j + W_{ij}u_{ij} + W_{hj}u_{hj} \tag{7.4}$$

where:

W_{ij} = the ratio of the sales of firm i to the total sales of the market observation for market j, i.e., S_{ij}/S_j and
W_{hj} = the ratio of the sales of firm h to the total sales of the market observation for market j, i.e., S_{hj}/S_j.

The market-related variable, M_j, needs no weighting, of course, as its value is the same for both firms. Calling the total error term of Equation (7.4) u_j, it follows from our assumptions in Chapter 2 that the expected value of u_j is zero:

$$E(u_j) = W_{ij}E(u_{ij}) + W_{hj}E(u_{hj})$$
$$= 0 + 0 \qquad (7.5)$$

The variance of u_j may be written:

$$V(u_j) = V(W_{ij}u_{ij}) + V(W_{hj}u_{hj}) + 2C[(W_{ij}u_{ij})(W_{hj}u_{hj})] \qquad (7.6)$$

Noting that $V(ax) = a^2 V(x)$ and that $C[(ax)(by)] = abC(xy)$ and employing the results from Chapter 2, the above equation can be written as:

$$V(u_j) = W_{ij}^2(\sigma_m^2 + \sigma_e^2) + W_{hj}^2(\sigma_m^2 + \sigma_e^2) + 2W_{ij}W_{hj}\sigma_m^2$$
$$= \sigma_m^2 + (W_{ij}^2 + W_{hj}^2)\sigma_e^2 \qquad (7.7)$$

On the assumption that the component variances σ_m^2 and σ_e^2 are constant, the error term for the industry observation will be heteroskedastic. This results from pooling independent firm-related error components. Because the market-related error components are the same for both firms, the pooling causes no reduction in market-related variance. On this observation, the expression in Equation (7.7) may be generalized to the case where the market rate of return is computed from the aggregate financial data of n specialized firms or divisons, as with the Census value added technique.

$$V(u_j) = \sigma_m^2 + \sum_{i=1}^{n} W_{ij}^2 \sigma_e^2 \qquad (7.8)$$

Because industry analysis would not, by definition, include more than one observation per industry, it can be shown that no autocorrelation exists; that is, $C(u_j u_k) = 0$ always. By this model, then, the omega matrix for industry analysis would be diagonal but the diagonal elements would be $K + \Sigma W_{ij}^2(1 - K)$ rather than 1's.[a] (Recall that $K = \sigma_m^2/\sigma_u^2$).

The degree of projected heteroskedasticity would depend in part upon the value of K and the variance or range in the value of the sum of the squared weights, ΣW_{ij}^2. Where K is large—most of the error is market related—the importance of the second and weighted term of the variance expression would be correspondingly small, of course, and heteroskedasticity would not be a real problem. Recall, however, that in industry analysis all firm-related variables are omitted.

As concerns the value of the sum of the squared weights, several possibilities should be noted. Use of Census data to construct industry rates of return will often result in a large number of specialized firms or divisions per observation. Though this will generally decrease the value of ΣW_{ij}^2, it may still allow a considerable range in individual values. In an industry where the shares of the two largest firms or divisions are, say, 60% and 20%, the minimum value of ΣW_{ij}^2 is greater than 0.40. If the two largest units control instead only 10% and 5% of the market, the maximum possible value of ΣW_{ij}^2 would be 0.055. Obviously, the existence of only a few specialized firms or divisions in some of the sample markets would enhance the probability of a heteroskedastic error term.

Where a sample rather than the population is used to derive the industry rate of return, W_{ij} *applies to the company share of sample rather than industry sales.* Given some value of K, then, the sampling approach could result in either more or less heteroskedasticity than the population approach. For instance, if one used the same number of firms to represent each industry and the firms within each group were of equal size, the variance term given in Equation (7.8) would be homoskedastic. More specifically, $V(u_j) = \sigma_m^2 + \sigma_e^2/n$ where n stands for number of firms per industry. The same result occurs where one uses a simple average of sample firm profit rates rather than aggregating their financial data for "industry" rate estimation and where one has an equal number of firms per observation.

Recall that the analysis of financial data from sectors legitimately allows for diversification of firms as long as each firm's products are contained within some sector's multimarket boundaries. For purposes of exposition, that assumption will be employed here. Though we could proceed again in the same manner as above—aggregating the data from hypothetical firms that are now possibly diversified—the additional algebra is of no particular value. For as long as division

---

[a] The market observation does not by definition include more than one division per firm. Adaptation of Model III will, therefore, not alter the configuration of the diagonal elements as $V(u_t) = \sigma_m^2 + \Sigma W_{ij}^2(\sigma_f^2 + \sigma_y^2)$ or $\sigma_u^2[K + \Sigma W_{ij}^2(1 - K)]$. Organization-related error could, of course, generate positive off-diagonal elements where divisions of the same firm are included in different market observations. These terms would be discounted heavily, however, by a term quite analogous to but much smaller than α_{ij} of the omega matrix for diversified firms.

independence is assumed, the results are invariant to whether one is aggregating firms or divisions, and we may proceed employing notation adopted directly above as well as some of the results.

Consider then, in addition to the observation on market j shown in Equation (7.4), another such observation for market k that is also made up of the ith and hth units (now either specialized firms or divisions). To form a sector observation, we group these two market observations together and call the total profits and sales of the sector P_T and S_T, respectively; that is,

$$P_T = P_j + P_k \tag{7.9}$$

$$S_T = S_j + S_k \tag{7.10}$$

Define:

Z_j = the ratio of the sales of market j to total sector sales, i.e., S_j/S_T.
Z_k = the ratio of the sales of market k to total sector sales, i.e., S_k/S_T.

Proceeding as before, the equation for the average profit rate of the sector, R_T, may be written as:

$$R_T = a + b(Z_k M_k + Z_j M_j) + Z_j u_j + Z_k u_k \tag{7.11}$$

Calling the total error term of Equation (7.11) g_T, it can be shown, employing the results of Equation (7.5), that the expected value of g_T is 0; that is:

$$\begin{aligned} E(g_T) &= Z_j E(u_j) + Z_k E(u_k) \\ &= 0 + 0 \end{aligned} \tag{7.12}$$

The variance of g_T may be written as:

$$V(g_T) = Z_j^2 V(u_j) + Z_k^2(u_k) + Z_j Z_k 2C(u_j u_k) \tag{7.13}$$

Substituting in the results derived in Equation (7.7) and noting that the covariance term is zero because no common market-related components are involved, we can write this term as:

$$V(g_T) = (Z_j^2 + Z_k^2)\sigma_m^2 + (Z_j^2 W_{ij}^2 + Z_j^2 W_{hj}^2 + Z_k^2 W_{ik}^2 + Z_k^2 W_{hk}^2)\sigma_e^2 \tag{7.14}$$

The term $Z_j W_{ij}$ is the ratio of sales by the ith firm or division of the jth market to total sector sales, that is, S_{ij}/S_T. Calling that ratio X_{ij} and then noting that $Z_j^2 W_{ij}^2 = X_{ij}^2$, we can readily generalize the results shown in Equation (7.14). It can be shown where there are m markets in a given sector, each being represented by up to n firms, that:

$$V(g_T) = \sum_{j=1}^{m} Z_j^2 \sigma_m^2 + \sum_{j=1}^{m} \sum_{i=1}^{n} X_{ij}^2 \sigma_e^2 \qquad (7.15)$$

Equation (7.15) indicates heteroskedasticity that results from the pooling of independent market-related error as well as firm-related error.[a] As concerns the apparent statistical importance of this result, several points are worth noting. Observations in sector analysis are always based more or less on the market populations rather than samples. Though X_{ij}, like W_{ij}, applies to the division's share, that share is now for sector rather than market sales and in general would be much smaller. This depends upon the level of aggregation, of course, which also affects the value of the Z_j's—that is, the market's share of sector sales. As noted previously, sector analysis has been carried out at two different levels—the SIC major group and the IRS minor industry. While the latter classification is much narrower and has been compared to the Census three-digit system, both major groups and minor industries are highly variable in the number of Census four-digit industries they embrace. Some of the IRS classifications represent only one four-digit industry group, which points out that the X_{ij}'s may not always be very small. With respect to the Z_j's, it should be noted that SIC major groups, for instance, may contain from four to well over thirty four-digit groups. This would allow considerable range in the magnitude of ΣZ_j^2.

Comanor and Wilson analyzed the effect of several structural variables on the profits of IRS minor industries using regression analysis. They observed that variance of the estimated residuals declined with increased size of the observation. Their conjecture that "smaller [IRS minor] industries may tend to have fewer firms so that the variance of average profit rates is larger" is certainly cogent in light of the above analysis.[1] Equation (7.15) would also pose the question of whether the smaller IRS groupings also represented fewer markets as well.

The derivations concerning the variance terms in market and sector studies also help elucidate the effects of aggregation on the relative strength of structure-profit relationships. As noted, in Chapter 1, others have observed that among industry and sector studies, the relationship of concentration to rate of return generally appears to be stronger at higher levels of aggregation. We suggested,

---

[a] Sector analysis makes it possible to include more than one division per firm in an observation. Application of Model III could, therefore, alter the configuration of the sector variance term shown in Equation (7.15) to $V(u_T) = \Sigma Z_j^2 \sigma_m^2 + \Sigma V_{ij}^2 \sigma_f^2 + \Sigma\Sigma X_{ij}^2 \sigma_e^2$, where V_{ij} equals each diversified firm's share of its sector's sales. The extent of heteroskedasticity is dampened in that f_i generates dependence between divisions of different markets but the same firm. The substance of our conclusions remains intact, however.

tentatively, that the explanation might center on the elimination of unexplained variance. On similar grounds, the FTC has indicated that attempting to explain variation among the rates of return for individual firms is "necessarily a more difficult task"[2] than explaining variation among the average rates for larger groups. We submit that these conclusions are not necessarily true. More specifically, it may be just as important in *what manner* one aggregates as well as *how much*.

In expanding on this proposition it is instructive to review some specific derivations. In Model II, which was judged appropriate for the analysis of diversified firm profits, the variance of the disturbance term was written:

$$V(g_{id}) = \Sigma D_{ij}^2(\sigma_m^2 + \sigma_e^2)$$

When this model was applied to industry analysis, the variance of the industry observation's error term, u_j, was shown to be:

$$V(u_j) = \sigma_m^2 + \Sigma W_{ij}^2 \sigma_e^2$$

And similarly, for the sector-related error term, g_T:

$$V(g_T) = \Sigma Z_j^2 \sigma_m^2 + \Sigma\Sigma X_{ij}^2 \sigma_e^2$$

All three equations indicate a reduction in unexplained variance relative to that which is associated with individual divisions or specialized firms. This is only one aspect of the problem but it is important. The other factor is the effect of aggregation on explained variance. Pursuing the matter of unexplained variance further, however, note that industry analysis would result in the reduction of only one component—the firm related—while multiproduct firm and sector equations indicate a reduction in variance of both components. An intuitive statement is perhaps appropriate. Market observations may average out extreme values associated with particular divisions while multimarket analysis, either *firm* or *sector*, may average out extreme values associated with particular *markets* as well.

By implication, multimarket observations could well lead to stronger results than would be observed with single market observations regardless of the level of aggregation. That is, regressions on individual diversified firms might show a stronger relationship between concentration and profits than would analysis where the same divisions were aggregated, instead, into market observations. The statement cannot be made unequivocally, however, as there is always the question of the effect of the different aggregative schemes on explained variance as well. Another factor is also the magnitude of K or the relative importance of market-related variance to the total. In other words, the issue at hand is an empirical one that cannot be settled on the basis of a priori reasoning.[a]

A fairly obvious conclusion at this point is that analyses using firm, industry, or sector observations will all be aggregative in one manner or another. Our original contention that it was the variance in the price-cost gaps of individual firms that is of intrinsic interest really applies to specialized firms or divisions. In any case, it should be borne in mind that all present researches provide analyses of the averages of micro relationships. The interpretation of the relative strength of the statistical results should be tempered accordingly.

One final observation bears mentioning before we leave the subject of aggregation. It concerns errors in measurement, a topic that we have ignored thus far and that is taken up only briefly now. Again we use the concentration-rate of return relationship as an example.

Consider the theoretical relationship $R_{ij} = BC_j + u_{ij}$, where C_j is the concentration ratio, R_{ij} is as before the rate of economic profit, and u_{ij} represents errors in the equation with all the characteristics of previous models. In view of the problems associated with delineation of theoretical markets in empirical work, one could anticipate problems in obtaining the conceptually correct concentration ratio and as a result encounter errors in measurement. Define c_j as the measured or observed concentration ratio and x_j as the error in measurement, so that $x_j = C_j - c_j$. As in the standard textbook case, we will assume that x_j has an expected value of zero and a finite variance σ_x^2.

One may still write an unbiased equation for the rate of profit and the *observable* concentration ratio by allowing for measurement error in the disturbance term:

$$R_{ij} = Bc_j + w_{ij} \qquad (7.16)$$

where $w_{ij} = Bx_j - u_{ij}$. By previous assumption $E(w_{ij}) = BE(x_j) - E(u_{ij}) = 0$. Application of least squares regression will still result in a biased estimate of B, however, because even though x_j may be distributed independently of C_j, it will be correlated with c_j, the variable actually used in the regression. If one assumes that x_j is also distributed independently of u_{ij} (for purposes of simplicity only), it can be

---

[a] No solid empirical proof can be brought to bear upon this matter because, for one thing, it is not empirically possible to regroup a given sample of diversified firms' divisions into market observations, or vice versa. Furthermore, any comparisons between the results of previous studies concerning diversified firms and those concerning single market observations would be futile because of the vast number of uncontrolled differences, including sample, rate of return, market definition, and the like. In searching for proof of their contentions, the FTC study disaggregated some previously tested market observations that had been constructed from data on "specialized firms." They missed the mark, however, for our discussion, as well as their own, implicitly concerns *diversified* firms versus market observations. The "specialized firms" which they used do not, of course, represent a pooling of market-related error, and the test is not applicable.

shown that the large sample expectation of the CLS estimated coefficient, b, of Equation (7.16) is: [3]

$$\text{plim } b = \frac{B}{1 + \sigma_x^2/\sigma_C^2} \quad \text{where plim stands for probability limit.} \quad (7.17)$$

The estimate b is biased downward from the population coefficient B by a factor related to the variance of the true value of the independent variable and the error in measurement.

The particular measurement error discussed here is obviously market related. For the multimarket observation, then, its variance could be reduced by pooling. Under the particular assumptions adopted above, it can be shown that the variance in measurement error associated with a diversified firm's weighted concentration ratio is $\Sigma D_{ij}^2 \sigma_x^2$. Whether this would decrease the bias, of course, depends on the effects of aggregation on the variance of the independent variable, which is probably also reduced to some extent. Cancellation of market-related measurement error through pooling is another possible reason, then, why multimarket observations (either firm or sector) might exhibit stronger results than single market observations.[a]

---

[a]The possibility also concerns division-related variables in the case of multimarket firm observations—for instance, the firm's weighted relative-size variable.

8 Major Findings

Consider a regression equation in which profit rate is expressed as a function of several "explanatory" variables. For the specialized firm we have proposed decomposing the error term into two component parts, one part attributable to the omission of market-related and the other firm-related variables. Suppose a random sample of specialized companies contains more than one firm from any one industry. It can be shown on the basis of simple assumptions that the error will display autocorrelation. If in addition we enrich our hypothetical world by allowing for diversified firms that represent mere aggregates of specialized "firms" or divisions, the error will display heteroskedasticity as well. A more general case which allows for interdependency among divisions within a diversified firm also implies a heteroskedastic, autocorrelated error term though the herteroskedasticity might not be as pronounced as in the simpler diversified firm model. As is well known, a heteroskedastic, autocorrelated error term implies that generalized least squares is the appropriate estimation procedure if the object is minimum-variance linear unbiased estimates. Though we have been mainly concerned with analysis of performance at the level of the firm, the error components analysis was applied to equations for industries and sectors. The results indicate the possibility of heteroskedastic error terms for these equations and suggest that the effects of aggregation might not be as clear-cut as some researchers have previously supposed.

The model which views the diversified firm as a mere aggregate of specialized divisions was applied in estimating structure-profit relationships. The empirical work on profit rates encompassed a considerable amount of sensitivity analysis. More particularly we have been concerned with the sensitivity of statistical results to (1) changes in statistical specifications, especially as regards the degree of autocorrelation, (2) alternative industry definitions, and (3) differing combinations of dependent and independent variables that seemed to be consistent with price theory. The investigation has been subject to numerous shortcomings. The sample of firms was not randomly chosen. Very likely, we have omitted important determinants from estimated equations that may be correlated with included variables. Quality of management relative to the industry average may be a good case in point. The variables that have been included are characterized by unknown margins of error. In terms of estimation, we have been handicapped by a lack of knowledge of certain variance ratios. As is common in this type of research, there has been a certain amount of experimentation with the data, a procedure that is scarcely in keeping with the theoretical underpinnings of statistical tests. What all this means is that our conclusions are tentative and fairly beg for replication in other sectors and/or time periods before generalizations are warranted. From another point of view, of course, our own study may be viewed as a replication of previous researches.

With this caveat in mind, the following results would appear to be of some interest. Our findings are wholly consistent with the hypothesis that concentration and product differentiation insulate firms from the full rigors of competition as evidenced by their ability to garner above-normal profits. The evidence for concentration is especially impressive. It almost seems that regardless of how one proceeds in terms of estimation procedure, industry definition, or choice of variables, concentration comes through with a positive sign and nearly always with a respectable t-ratio. In addition we have been unable to find any evidence that the relationship is other than linear continuous. As regards the best measure of concentration, it appeared that the results were insensitive to the use of several measures including the two, three, four, and eight largest firm ratios, whereas the marginal concentration ratios proposed by Miller did not appear to be meaningful measures of structure.

Unfortunately, the estimated coefficients for concentration vary among formulations. For illustration, consider the GLS estimates given in Table 5-1 and assume that a firm in an industry with a four-firm concentration ratio equal to 0.5 incurs no advertising or R and D expense. A 10% increase in concentration would tend to increase profit over sales by between 12% and 40%. While researchers have occasionally been able to produce either negative or insignificant coefficients for concentration, the bulk of the studies show, as Stigler has noted, weak but positive relationships.[1] The present study provides still more evidence to add to the heap.

While our results tend to confirm the product differentiation hypothesis, it is very difficult to assign much meaning to the magnitudes of the coefficients for the two variables involved—namely, advertising and R and D both expressed as ratios to sales. The reason for this is simply that these two variables are intended as proxies for the extent of product differentiation. Indeed, we have been unable to measure product differentiation per se, let alone the impacts that it might have on rates of profit. What we can do, though, is illustrate the differences in expected profit rates as between a firm in a highly competitive industry and another in a highly monopolistic industry. Let the four-firm concentration ratio, advertising rate, and R and D rate equal, respectively, 0.10, 0.005, and 0.001 for a competitive industry and 0.80, 0.04, and 0.03 for a monopolistic industry. Using reconstructed census industries and setting the omega ratio at 0.5, we find that the competitive firm's excess profit is roughly zero whereas the monopolistic firm's excess would amount to roughly 5% of sales. Alternatively, use the fourth equation from Table 5-4. The competitive firm's after-tax profit amounts to roughly 4% of net worth whereas the corresponding figure for the monopolistic firm is 16%

The *t*-ratios for advertising and R and D improve as industry definitions become, according to our judgment, more crude. If in point of fact the Census four-digit or Census four-five digit industries meet more closely the economic criteria for industry definition than do our own reconstructed census definitions, the evidence for the product differentiation hypothesis is far stronger than we have been inclined to believe.

Turning to the remaining variables, relative firm size appeared to be a very strong variable. As noted, we have reservations regarding the theoretical rationale for including this variable and would urge further investigation, particularly in nonfood sectors. Absolute firm size, plant scale barriers to entry, and diversification did not yield much of interest. The rationale for including these variables is not firm and our measurements have been crude. Our feeling is that the importance of some of these variables in "explaining" variance in company profit rates has been overrated in some of the previous econometric research.

Before leaving our results on the structure-profit relationship, it is well worth noting their remarkable consistency with those reported by the FTC for a similar sample of firms for an earlier time period. Some differences in results did occur, of course, and there appear to be a large number of plausible explanations for these differences in light of differing estimation procedures, industry definitions, measurements, and the like. Suffice it here to say that both studies provide similar conclusions regarding concentration, product differentiation, relative and absolute firm size, and company diversification. (The FTC did not analyze, to our knowledge, the plant scale barrier to entry and its impacts on profit rates.)

The major findings regarding the association between technological change and structure in the food sector can be summarized with dispatch. Concentration appears to be positively related to the rate of R and D expenditure (or patenting), and the *t*-ratios tend to be very high. The Schumpeter hypothesis is given rather substantial support. Nelson's hypothesis regarding the positive effect of diversification on investment in technological change appears also to have been supported. The neo-Schumpeterian hypothesis that bigness in and of itself begets R and D expenditures is not supported. Product differentiation does not appear to contribute to technological change. All and all, our findings on the relationship between structure and progress are happily consistent with the previous research findings as summarized by Scherer (as previously cited). While some hypotheses are supported and others are not, it is always possible that the hypotheses in question are of limited importance. In particular it may well be that the nonstructural determinants of technological change in the economy at large dwarfs market structure in terms of importance. Differing technological opportunities among sectors and the general increase in levels of education come readily to mind as examples of nonstructural determinants.

We must confess a certain amount of satisfaction with out statistical models in the estimation of structure-profit relationships. In particular, the patterns of residuals under various alternative formulations are consistent with the a priori predictions concerning heteroskedasticity. The schemes used by previous researchers to deal with heteroskedasticity are ad hoc in nature relative to those proposed here, and the problem of autocorrelation seems to have been overlooked completely. We feel that at the very least, some of the impressive statistical findings reported by other researchers who have placed heavy reliance on classical least squares merit reappraisal. Recall that generalized least squares with positive omega ratios led to t-ratios substantially lower than those obtained from classical least squares.

The performance of our statistical models in the examination of structure-progress relationships, on the other hand, has been at best disheartening. Though division and market orientation of progressiveness may be weaker than in the case of profits, the perverse pattern of heteroskedasticity obviously raises questions about our entire approach. We are unaware that this pattern of heteroskedasticity has been observed in previous researches, however, and there is always the possibility that we have come across a statistical aberration. This unsatisfactory state of affairs would appear to make a plea for further work felicitous.

The results of sensitivity analysis regarding industry definition appear to support our early concern that Census four-digit industries are simply too gross for use in cross-section research. If the food sector is at all representative of manufacturing generally, the reliance placed on Census four-digit industries may be causing much mischief in the search for structure-performance relationships. The implication is that greater efforts should be made in cross-section research to define industries with greater care.

As a final thought, this monograph points up vividly the subjectivity that is involved in nearly every stage of cross-section research on structure-performance relationships. How should the researcher define industries, choose samples, decide on the level of aggregation, identify and measure relevant variables, choose the form of equation, pick an estimation procedure, and so on and so on. In our view, what is needed is not so much *more* studies as *more careful* studies. In this connection it is hoped that the present monograph will be helpful in further work. Surely it has raised issues that cannot be swept under the rug if further progress is to be made.

Appendix A

This appendix contains three tables, each corresponding to a different set of industry definitions and providing structural and other data.

Table A-1
Reconstructed Census Industries: Four-Firm and Eight-Firm Concentration Percentages, 1963, and Market Growth Rates, 1954–1963

Industry	Census Code Description	Four-Firm Concentration (M_{1j})	Eight-Firm Concentration	Market Growth Rate (M_{3j})
1. Animal feed, manufactured for commercial animals	2042 minus 20423	21	28	2.0
2. Baby food in cans and jars	20321	95	99	7.6
3. Baked goods, dry, crackers	20521	71	81	4.3
4. Baked goods, dry, cookies	20522	52	60	4.4
5. Baked goods, soft[a]	2051	40	57	2.5
6. Baking powder and yeast	20994	86	91	1.5
7. Beans, canned dry	20323 minus (20323–86, –91)[b]	65	77	3.5
8. Brewing	2082	33	51	3.6
9. Chips, potato, corn, and miscellaneous flour products	20992	41	51	11.7
10. Confections, bars, and specialties	20711 plus 20712 plus (20722–32, –35, –37, –51) plus (20716–81, –82, –83, –87)	25	34	2.6
11. Confections, bulk and packaged candy	20713 plus 20714 plus (20722–42, –47) plus (20716–84, –85)	40	52	2.4
12. Cereal, ready to eat	(20430–11, –12, –15, –17, –19)	90	99	7.3
13. Cereal, to be cooked	(20430–52, –53, –59)	80	92	1.1
14. Chocolate manufacturing	2072	71	83	2.4
15. Coffee	2095	54	70	5.0
16. Distilling, raw grain spirits	20851	48	62	2.4

APPENDIX A

#	Description	Code		
17.	Distilling, beverages, blended and bottled	20853	48	2.4
18.	Dessert mixes	20991	86	5.7
19.	Fish and seafood	c	58	1.7
20.	Fish and seafood, fresh and frozen finfish	(20361–11, –12, –14) plus 20362-13	23	9.9
21.	Fish and seafood, fresh, frozen, and canned shellfish	(20361–16, –17) plus 20362-15 plus (Shellfish, total in SIC 2031, Dept. of Int. figures)	26	9.9
22.	Flavorings and extracts	20871	27	6.0
23.	Flavorings for soft drink bottlers	20872	89	4.6
24.	Fruit, canned and frozen	20331 plus (20371–35, –41, –51, –55, –69)	35	3.7
25.	Fruit, dried	(20341–13, –15, –17, –18, –21, –29)	39	6.8
26.	Grain mill products, wheat flour	2041 minus 20415	40	-0.8
27.	Grain mill products, mixes and prepared flours	[20415 minus (20415-71, –73, –75, –79)] plus [20455 minus (20455-71, –73, –75, –79)]	70	2.6
28.	Grain mill products, refrigerated doughs	(20415–71, –73, –75, –79) plus (20455-71, –73, –75, –79)	87	2.4
29.	Gum, chewing	2073 minus 20730-15	90	2.0
30.	Juice, noncarbonated fruit and vegetable	20334 plus 20335 plus (20371–81, –82, –83, –85, –86, –87, –90, –91, –92, –95, –00) plus (20860–91, –93)	31	10.3
31.	Meat and poultry, fresh and processed	2011 plus 2013 plus [2015 minus 20156]	25	3.6
32.	Meat sauces, all types, excluding catsup	(20353–11, –51)	45	9.5
33.	Milk, canned evaporated and condensed	(20232–12, –16)	70	-2.6
34.	Milk, dried instant	d	73	1.2

Table A-1, continued

Industry	Census Code Description	Four-firm Concentration (M_{1j})	Eight-Firm Concentration	Market Growth Rate (M_{3j})
35. Milk, fluid and dairy products[a]	2026 minus 20261	59	74	5.4
36. Margarine and butter	2021 plus 20962	14	20	-0.8
37. Nuts, shelled and salted	(20716-11, -31, -51)	21	36	6.7
38. Oils, crude edible	d	32	42	4.7
39. Oils, refined edible	2096 minus 20962	51	74	3.8
40. Peanut butter	20999-45	51	77	6.2
41. Pet food	20423	43	57	10.0
42. Pickles	[20352 minus 20352-61] plus 20353-71	20	31	5.9
43. Protein meals	d	51	68	7.5
44. Salad dressing, prepared	20354	57	67	2.3
45. Soup, all forms	Canned soup from (20322, 20324, and 20320) plus 20342	92	96	3.5

APPENDIX A

46. Spices	(20999-31, -33, -38, -39)	70	80	7.9
47. Sweeteners for human consumption	2062 plus [2063 minus 20630] plus (20460-08, -12, -13, -14, -16, -17, -18)	44	64	2.6
48. Tobacco, cigars	2121	59	71	5.5
49. Tobacco, cigarettes	2111	80	100	0.0
50. Tomato products, catsup	(20336-33, -39)	81	94	5.1
51. Tomato products, for cooking	20336 minus (20336-33, -39)	46	68	6.5
52. Vegetables, canned and frozen	[20332 minus (20332-52, -54, -73, -74, -75)] plus 20341-39 plus [20372 minus 20372-47]	29	41	5.5
53. Vinegar	20996 minus 20996-11	49	60	6.4
54. Wet corn milling	2046	65	87	1.7

[a] Consider the average weighted concentration ratio, either the four-firm or the eight-firm, for the various regional milk (soft-baked goods) markets of the ith "dairy" ("soft-baked goods") company. The concentration ratio in the table is the average of that figure for all "dairy" ("soft-baked goods") companies in the sample. Figures for M_{3j} represent similar averages. The values of these variables vary for individual companies due to the location of their markets. The sample averages are quite representative of the firm figures, however.

[b] Parentheses designate a series of seven-digit Census codes which all fall in the same five-digit product class. The five-digit product class is given only once at the beginning of the series. In this particular case, for instance, (20323-86, -91) represents Census codes 20323-86 and 20323-91.

[c] Finfish and Shellfish totals as reported in SIC 2031, Department of Interior figures.

[d] There are no appropriate Census aggregates.

Source: See Chapters 3 and 4.

Table A-2
Census Four-Digit Industries: Four-Firm and Eight-Firm Concentration Percentages, 1963; Market Shares of Minimum-Optimum Sized Plants, 1963; and Market Growth Rates, 1958–1963

Industry	Census Code	Four-Firm Concentration Percentage (M_{1j})	Eight-Firm Concentration Percentage	Plant Share (M_{2j})	Market Growth Rate (M_{3j})
1. Meat slaughtering plant products	2011	30	40	0.001	0.9
2. Sausages and other prepared meat products	2013	14	21	0.38	3.8
3. Poultry dressing plant products	2015	13	19	0.25	4.0
4. Creamery butter	2021	8	14	0.04	0.4
5. Natural and processed cheese	2022	45	50	0.09	7.0
6. Condensed and evaporated milk	2023	33	42	1.08	2.0
7. Ice cream and ices	2024	34	43	0.10	1.3
8. Fluid milk	2026	22	29	0.003	1.5
9. Canned and cured seafoods including soup, except frozen	2031	33	47	0.10	0.9
10. Canned specialties	2032	69	79	1.87	2.7
11. Canned fruits, vegetables, preserves, jams, and jellies	2033	24	35	0.17	3.4
12. Dried and dehydrated food products	2034	35	51	0.57	3.8
13. Pickled fruits and vegetables; vegetable sauces and seasonings; salad dressings	2035	29	40	0.91	4.5
14. Fresh or frozen packaged fish	2036	23	34	0.14	5.7
15. Frozen fruits, fruit sauces, vegetables, and specialties	2037	23	36	0.07	9.8
16. Flour and other grain mill products	2041	36	51	0.15	1.6
17. Prepared foods for animals and fowls	2042	22	29	0.01	3.6
18. Cereal preparations	2043	82	94	6.52	5.4

APPENDIX A

19. Wet corn milling	2046	65	87	2.80	2.6
20. Bread and other bakery products except biscuit, crackers and pretzels	2051	22	34	0.09	1.5
21. Biscuit, crackers, and pretzels	2052	58	66	0.05	3.0
22. Refined cane sugar and by-products Refined beet sugar and by-products	2062 plus 2063	45[a]	65[a]	1.02	5.6
23. Candy and other confectionery products	2071	15	26	0.60	3.5
24. Chocolate and cocoa products	2072	71	83	1.58	1.7
25. Chewing gum and chewing gum base	2073	86	95	4.20	3.4
26. Malt liquors and brewing by-products	2082	34	52	1.32[b]	3.0
27. Wines, brandy, and brandy spirits	2084	50	63	0.43[b]	3.8
28. Distilled, rectified, and blended liquors	2085	56	73	2.09	3.5
29. Bottled and canned soft drinks	2086	11	16	0.07	8.0
30. Flavorings, extracts and flavoring sirups, nec.	2087	55	63	1.14	8.6
31. Cottonseed oil mill products Soybean oil mills Vegetable oil mills, except cottonseed and soybean	2091 plus 2092 plus 2093	32[a]	45[a]	0.02	5.6
32. Roasted coffee	2095	54	70	0.03	-2.0
33. Shortening, table oils, margarine, and other edible fats and oils	2096	41	63	0.29	0.7
34. Food preparations, nec.	2099	26	35	0.05	6.0
35. Cigarettes	2111	82[a]	100	0.10[b]	3.8
36. Cigars	2121	59	81	0.71[b]	0.1

[a]Estimated on the basis of primary and Census data
[b]Field survey estimates

Source: U.S. Congress, Senate Committee on the Judiciary. *Concentration Ratios in Manufacturing Industry 1963: Part I With Individual Views.* Bureau of the Census for the Subcommittee on Antitrust and Monopoly, Senate 99th Congress, 2nd Session. (Washington, D.C.: Government Printing Office, May, 1966).

Table A-3
Census Four-Five-Digit Industries: Four-Firm and Eight-Firm Concentration Percentages, 1963, and Market Growth Rates, 1958–1963

Industry	Census Code	Four-Firm Concentration Percentage (M_{1j})	Eight-Firm Concentration Percentage	Market Growth Rate (M_{3j})
1. Meat slaughtering plant products	2011	30	40	0.9
2. Sausages and other prepared meat products	2013	14	21	3.8
3. Poultry dressing plant products	2015	13	19	4.0
4. Creamery butter	2021	8	14	0.4
5. Dry milk products	20231	22	30	3.7
6. Canned milk	20232	66	78	0.6
7. Ice cream and ices	2024	34	43	1.3
8. Bottled milk and cream	20262	25	32	0.8
9. Canned and cured seafoods	2031	33	47	0.9
10. Canned baby foods, except meat	20321	95	99	4.5
11. Soups and other canned specialties and canned specialties, nsk.	20322 20324 20320	84	89	3.7
12. Canned dry beans	20323	44	63	3.7
13. Canned fruits	20331	37	52	2.4
14. Canned vegetables, except hominy and mushrooms	20332	34	41	4.7
15. Canned fruit juices	20334	31	43	5.3
16. Canned vegetable juices	20335	55	69	-0.5
17. Catsup and other tomato sauces	20336	49	63	3.9
18. Jams, jellies, and preserves	20338	31	44	2.8
19. Dried and dehydrated fruits and vegetables and freezer-dried products except soups	20341	35	51	3.9

APPENDIX A

20. Pickles and other pickled products	20352	23	34	5.3
21. Meat sauces (except tomato) and unfinished pickles	20353	45	57	8.6
22. Salad dressings[a]	20354	57	67	3.0
23. Fresh or frozen packaged fish	2036	23	34	5.7
24. Frozen fruits, juices, and ades	20371	28	42	4.1
25. Frozen vegetables	20372	39	56	11.4
26. Wheat flour, except blended or prepared	20411	40	58	0.9
27. Prepared flour and flour mixes	20415 plus 20455	60[b]	75[b]	-3.1
28. Prepared foods for animals and fowls	2042	22	29	3.6
29. Dog and cat food	20423	42	56	7.7
30. Cereal preparations	20430	82	94	5.4
31. Wet corn milling	20460	65	87	2.6
32. Bread and other bakery products except biscuit, crackers, and pretzels	2051	22	34	1.9
33. Biscuit, crackers, and pretzels	20521	71	81	5.2
34. Other "dry" bakery products	20522	52	60	1.9
35. Refined cane sugar and by-products Refined beet sugar and by-products	20620 plus 20630	45[a]	65[a]	5.6
36. Bar goods	20711	48	61	1.6
37. 5¢ and 10¢ specialties	20712	51	65	4.5
38. Package goods	20713	24	36	5.5
39. Bulk goods	20714	26	38	-0.5
40. Salted nuts and other confectionery-type products	20716	28	40	6.3
41. Chocolate and cocoa products	2072	71	83	1.7
42. Confectionery-type chocolate made from cocoa beans	20722[b]	90	98	4.9

Table A-3, continued

Industry	Census Code	Four-Firm Concentration Percentage (M_{1j})	Eight-Firm Concentration Percentage	Market Growth Rate (M_{3j})
43. Chewing gum and chewing gum base	20730	86	95	3.4
44. Malt liquors and brewing by-products	20820	34	52	3.0
45. Distilled liquor except brandy	20851	51	76	2.4
46. Bottled liquors	20853	58	75	3.7
47. Bottled and canned soft drinks	20860	11	16	8.0
48. Flavoring extracts, emulsions, and other liquid flavors	20871	27	36	6.8
49. Flavoring sirups for use by soft drink bottlers	20873	90[b]	91	6.6
50. Cottonseed oil mill products Soybean oil mills Vegetable oil mills, except cottonseed and soybean	2091 plus 2092 plus 2093	32[a]	45[a]	5.6
51. Roasted coffee	2095	54	70	-2.0
52. Shortening, table oils, margarine, and other edible fats and oils	2096	41	63	0.7
53. Shortening and cooking oils	20961	51	74	0.3
54. Margarine	20962	50	73	1.8
55. Desserts	20991	86	92	6.7
56. Chips	20992	41	51	9.6
57. Sweetening sirups and molasses	20993	63	76	7.4
58. Baking powder and yeast	20994	86	91	-1.0
59. Vinegar and cider	20996	49	60	4.0
60. Other food preparations, nec.	20999	23	34	4.1
61. Cigarettes	2111	82[a]	100	3.8
62. Cigars	2121	59	81	0.1

[a] The data are for 1958.
[b] Estimated from Primary and Census data.

Source: See source for Table A-2.

Appendix B

Appendix B contains six tables that give greater detail on regression results plus other information.

Table B-1
Four-Firm Weighted Concentration Ratios for Ninety-nine Food Processing Companies, Ranked Using Reconstructed Census Industry Definitions with Corresponding Figures for Census Four-Digit and Four-Five-Digit Definitions

Reconstructed Census	Census Four-Five Digit	Census Four Digit	Reconstructed Census	Census Four-Five Digit	Census Four Digit
.95	.94	.69	.59	.59	.59
.90	.81	.82	.58	.58	.57
.90	.85	.86	.56	.33	.32
.85	.84	.67	.56	.56	.42
.84	.42	.35	.55	.56	.39
.81	.82	.82	.54	.70	.71
.80	.80	.82	.53	.28	.24
.79	.80	.81	.53	.27	.24
.79	.80	.81	.53	.49	.37
.77	.73	.61	.52	.58	.32
.75	.37	.32	.51	.25	.24
.73	.60	.46	.51	.45	.45
.72	.30	.22	.50	.44	.34
.70	.22	.26	.49	.21	.22
.66	.64	.46	.48	.56	.56
.65	.64	.46	.48	.56	.56
.65	.64	.46	.48	.53	.56
.63	.58	.45	.48	.56	.56
.63	.62	.58	.48	.56	.56
.60	.38	.30	.48	.56	.56
.60	.55	.46	.45	.42	.34
.59	.27	.25	.45	.21	.22
.59	.41	.28	.44	.44	.45
.59	.36	.25	.44	.44	.45
.59	.44	.45	.44	.44	.45
.44	.21	.22	.33	.33	.34
.44	.44	.45	.33	.33	.34
.44	.44	.45	.33	.33	.34
.44	.44	.45	.31	.28	.25
.44	.44	.45	.31	.28	.27
.43	.43	.32	.30	.28	.22
.42	.44	.45	.30	.29	.30
.42	.42	.43	.29	.38	.23
.42	.21	.22	.29	.33	.24
.42	.44	.45	.29	.38	.37
.40	.47	.15	.29	.31	.25
.40	.21	.22	.27	.31	.30
.40	.39	.36	.26	.25	.15
.40	.37	.34	.25	.40	.38
.39	.21	.22	.25	.28	.30
.38	.21	.22	.25	.24	.30
.38	.38	.35	.25	.29	.30
.38	.38	.35	.25	.29	.30
.37	.37	.27	.25	.22	.30
.37	.37	.34	.25	.29	.30
.36	.36	.35	.25	.27	.30
.35	.36	.24	.25	.29	.30
.33	.33	.34	.23	.22	.23
.33	.33	.34	.22	.19	.16
.33	.33	.34			

Table B-2
Ninety-nine Food Sector Companies: Estimated Regression Equations Relating Total Returns to All Assets (R'_i) to Three Explanatory Variables Using Classical Least Squares (CLS) and Using Generalized Least Squares (GLS) with Three Alternative Specifications of the Variance-Covariance Matrix of the Error Term and Using Alternative Industry Definitions

		Regression Coefficients with t-ratios in Parentheses			
Estimation Procedure	Intercept	Four-Firm Concentration Ratio (M_{ij})	Advertising Expenditures over Sales (Y_{1i})	Research and Development Expenditures over Sales (Y_{2i})	Coefficient of Multiple Determination (R^2)
		Reconstructed Census Industry Definitions			
CLS	0.0640	0.1047 (2.30)	0.6433 (2.62)	1.4431 (1.93)	.277
GLS: 0.0	0.0475	0.1325 (2.56)	0.6361 (2.29)	1.5496 (1.65)	.848
GLS: 0.5	0.0050	0.2228 (2.76)	0.4280 (1.22)	1.1883 (1.01)	.588
GLS: 0.8	−0.0711	0.3596 (3.32)	0.4067 (1.04)	0.5695 (0.40)	.359

APPENDIX B

		Census Four-Five-Digit Industry Definitions		
CLS	0.0720	0.0867 (2.08)	0.7636 (3.40)	1.8405 (2.62)	.270
GLS: 0.0	0.0769	0.0796 (1.86)	0.7852 (2.93)	1.8429 (1.97)	.844
GLS: 0.5	0.0609	0.1294 (1.90)	0.5949 (1.71)	1.8911 (1.65)	.571
GLS: 0.8	0.0413	0.1630 (1.66)	0.5767 (1.41)	1.7511 (1.25)	.337
		Census Four-Digit Industry Definitions		
CLS	0.0837	0.0566 (1.31)	0.8527 (3.83)	2.0780 (2.98)	.250
GLS: 0.0	0.0780	0.0795 (1.65)	0.8376 (3.20)	2.0875 (2.28)	.842
GLS: 0.5	0.0613	0.1404 (1.85)	0.6374 (1.86)	2.0733 (1.83)	.570
GLS: 0.8	0.0402	0.1796 (1.63)	0.6217 (1.53)	1.9346 (1.39)	.336

Table B-3
Ninety-nine Food Sector Companies: Estimated Regression Equations Relating Profit over Net Worth (R_i'') to Three Explanatory Variables Using Classical Least Squares (CLS) and Using Generalized Least Squares (GLS) with Three Alternative Specifications of the Variance-Covariance Matrix of the Error Term and Using Alternative Industry Definitions

		Regression Coefficients with t-ratios in Parentheses			
Estimation Procedure	Intercept	Four-Firm Concentration Ratio (M_{ij})	Advertising Expenditures over Sales (Y_{1i})	Research and Development Expenditures over Sales (Y_{2i})	Coefficient of Multiple Determination (R^2)
		Reconstructed Census Industry Definitions			
CLS	0.0400	0.0865 (2.81)	0.0450 (2.43)	0.9284 (1.83)	.301
GLS: 0.0	0.0367	0.0875 (2.63)	0.4990 (2.80)	1.0947 (1.82)	.847
GLS: 0.5	0.0219	0.1114 (2.08)	0.4955 (2.13)	1.044 (1.34)	.621
GLS: 0.8	−0.0196	0.1751 (2.37)	0.5610 (2.11)	0.8141 (0.85)	.399

APPENDIX B

		Census Four-Five-Digit Industry Definitions		
CLS	0.0585	0.0380 (1.31)	1.3719 (2.81)	.256
GLS: 0.0	0.0612	0.0347 (1.24)	1.3955 (2.29)	.867
GLS: 0.5	0.0519	0.0586 (1.30)	1.4131 (1.87)	.609
GLS: 0.8	0.0340	0.0828 (1.27)	1.381 (1.48)	.374
		Census Four-Digit Industry Definitions		
CLS	0.0627	0.0277 (0.93)	1.4729 (3.06)	.249
GLS: 0.0	0.0626	0.0312 (1.00)	1.5121 (2.55)	.867
GLS: 0.5	0.0530	0.0602 (1.20)	1.4997 (2.00)	.608
GLS: 0.8	0.0343	0.0882 (1.20)	1.4871 (1.60)	.373

Table B-4

Ninety-nine Food Sector Companies: Estimated Regression Equations Relating Profit over Sales (R_i) to Four Explanatory Variables Using Classical Least Squares (CLS) and Using Generalized Least Squares (GLS) with One Specification of the Variance-Covariance Matrix of the Error Term, Concentration Based on Alternative Industry Definitions

Estimation Procedure	Intercept	Regression Coefficients with t-ratios in Parentheses				Coefficient of Multiple Determination (R^2)
		Four-Firm Concentration Ratio (M_{1j})	Advertising Expenditures over Sales (Y_{1i})	R and D Expenditures over Sales (Y_{2i})	Four-Digit Optimum Plant Size Barrier (M_{2j})	
		Concentration: Reconstructed Census Industries				
CLS	0.0081	0.0343 (3.11)	0.1619 (2.58)	0.6319 (3.51)	0.2949 (1.62)	.474
GLS: 0.5	−0.0146	0.0474 (2.55)	0.1162 (1.43)	0.5477 (2.13)	0.3571 (1.07)	.435
		Concentration: Census Four-Digit Industries				
CLS	0.0009	0.0105 (0.88)	0.2438 (4.15)	0.8466 (4.82)	0.3129 (1.48)	.425
GLS: 0.5	−0.0002	0.0217 (1.03)	0.1728 (2.16)	0.7467 (2.97)	0.3496 (0.86)	.402
		Concentration: Reconstructed Census Product Categories—Nat. Mkts.				
CLS	−0.0064	0.0333 (3.03)	0.1614 (2.55)	0.6287 (3.46)	0.2463 (1.32)	.472
GLS: 0.5	−0.0043	0.0315 (1.85)	0.1199 (1.42)	0.6095 (2.34)	0.3285 (0.93)	.417

Table B-5
Ninety-nine Food Sector Companies: Estimated Regression Equations Relating Profit over Sales (R_i) to Combinations of Five Independent Explanatory Variables Using Classical Least Squares (CLS) and Using Generalized Least Squares (GLS) with Three Alternative Specifications of the Variance-Covariance Matrix of Error Terms, Reconstructed Census Industries

		Regression Coefficients with t-ratios in Parentheses					
Estimation Procedure	Intercept	Four-Firm Concentration Ratio (M_{1j})	Advertising Expenditures over Sales (Y_{1i})	R and D Expenditures over Sales (Y_{2i})	Relative Firm Size (Y_{3i})	Four-Digit Optimum Plant Size Barrier (M_{2j})	Coefficient of Multiple Determination (R^2)
CLS	−0.0099	0.0319 (2.84)	0.1880 (3.21)	0.6399 (3.59)	0.0197 (1.91)		.479
GLS: 0.0	−0.0143	0.0366 (3.25)	0.1939 (3.23)	0.6712 (3.32)	0.0160 (1.85)		.705
GLS: 0.5	−0.0231	0.0514 (3.00)	0.1092 (1.44)	0.4865 (1.94)	0.0269 (2.71)		.469
GLS: 0.8	−0.0359	0.0705 (3.06)	0.0311 (1.04)	0.0549 (0.64)	0.0320 (3.16)		.322
CLS	−0.0097	0.0276 (2.45)	0.1475 (2.38)	0.5945 (3.34)	0.0214 (2.08)	0.3274 (1.83)	.498
GLS: 0.5	−0.0212	0.0439 (2.45)	0.0736 (0.92)	0.4790 (1.92)	0.0283 (2.84)	0.4423 (1.39)	.480

Table B-6
Ninety-nine Food Sector Companies: Estimated Regression Equations Relating Profit over Sales (R_i) to Combinations of Five Independent Explanatory Variables Using Classical Least Squares (CLS) and Using Generalized Least Squares (GLS) with Three Alternative Specifications of the Variance-Covariance Matrix of the Error Term, Census Four-Digit Industries

		Regression Coefficients with t-ratios in Parentheses					
Estimation Procedure	Intercept	Four-Firm Concentration Ratio (M_{1j})	Advertising Expenditures over Sales (Y_{1i})	R and D Expenditures over Sales (Y_{2i})	Relative Firm Size (Y_{3i})	Four-Digit Optimum Plant Size Barrier (M_{2j})	Coefficient of Multiple Determination (R^2)
CLS	−0.0061	0.0196 (1.93)	0.2165 (3.92)	0.8798 (5.37)	0.0308 (3.33)		.479
GLS: 0.0	−0.0082	0.0274 (2.68)	0.1837 (3.07)	0.8118 (4.21)	0.0283 (3.52)		.709
GLS: 0.5	−0.0090	0.0362 (2.62)	0.1142 (1.49)	0.7436 (3.12)	0.0262 (3.17)		.456
GLS: 0.8	−0.0144	0.0478 (2.06)	0.0481 (0.53)	0.6291 (2.16)	0.0277 (3.26)		.281
CLS	−0.0043	0.0116 (1.02)	0.1866 (3.19)	0.8274 (4.96)	0.0304 (3.32)	0.2967 (1.47)	.486
GLS: 0.5	−0.0059	0.0271 (1.08)	0.0823 (1.02)	0.0271 (3.02)	0.0271 (3.27)	0.4637 (1.19)	.464

Notes

Introduction

1. Marshall Hall and Leonard Weiss, "Firm Size and Profitability," *Review of Economics and Statistics*, Vol. 49 (Aug., 1967), pp. 319-331; and Federal Trade Commission, *Economic Report on the Influence of Market Structure on the Profit Performance of Food Manufacturing Companies*, Staff Report, Washington, D.C., U.S. Government Printing Office, Sept., 1969. The Federal Trade Commission study will hereafter be referred to as the FTC study.

Chapter 1

1. Edward S. Mason, *Economic Concentration and the Monopoly Problem* (Cambridge: Harvard University Press, 1957), p. 62.
2. In this connection we applaud, heartily, Grether's suggestion for research geared toward bringing industrial organization and behavioral theories into better working relationships. See E. T. Grether, "Industrial Organization," *American Economic Review*, 60 (May, 1970), pp. 83-89.
3. See A. C. Johnson and Peter Helmberger, "Elasticity of Demand as an Element of Market Structure," *American Economic Review*, 57 (Dec., 1967), pp. 1218-1221.
4. See F. M. Sherer, "Firm Size and Patented Inventions," *American Economic Review*, 55 (Dec., 1965) pp. 1097-1125, and David R. Kamerchen, "The Influence of Ownership and Control on Profit Rates," *Review*, 55 (Dec., 1965), pp. 1097-1125.
5. For a review of many of these studies, see Norman R. Collins and Lee E. Preston, *Concentration and Price-Cost Margins in Manufacturing Industries*, (Berkeley: University of California Press, 1968), pp. 18-44. See also William S. Comanor and Thomas A. Wilson, "Advertising, Market Structure and Performance," *Review of Economics and Statistics*, 49 (Nov., 1967), pp. 432-440; and Richard A. Miller, "Marginal Concentration Ratios and Industrial Profit Rates: Some Empirical Results of Oligopoly Behavior," *The Southern Economic Journal*, 34 (Oct., 1967), pp. 259-267.
6. See Joe S. Bain, "Relation of Profit Rate to Industry Concentration: American Manufacturing, 1936-1940." *Quarterly Journal of Economics*, 65 (Aug., 1951), pp. 293-324; and George J. Stigler, "A Theory of Oligopoly," *Journal of Political Economy*, 72 (Feb., 1964), pp. 44-61.
7. See Collins and Preston, pp. 54-57; and David Schwartzman, "The Effect of Monopoly on Price," *Journal of Political Economy*, 67 (Aug., 1959), pp. 252-262.
8. See Comanor and Wilson, and George J. Stigler, *Capital and Rates of Return in Manufacturing Industries* (Princeton: Princeton University Press, 1963), p. 209.

9. John M. Blair, "An Overview of Conglomerate Concentration." *Economics of Conglomerate Growth* (Oregon State University, Agricultural Research Foundation, 1969). Blair indicates that the average of "primarily engaged in" to "with plants in" for the top 200 is about 1:6 (p.7). Individual major group ratios are also given (p. 8).
10. Bain, *Industrial Organization,* 2nd ed. (New York: John Wiley & Sons, Inc., 1968), pp. 444–445.
11. George J. Stigler, *The Organization of Industry* (Homewood: Richard D. Irwin, Inc., 1968), pp. 145–146; and Collins and Preston, p. 48.
12. Bain, pp. 449–451.
13. See the studies by Hall and Weiss, Federal Trade Commission, and David R. Kamerschen.
14. See Hall and Weiss, pp. 223–224.
15. E. T. Grether, p. 85.

Chapter 2

1. An alternative rationalization of errors in the equation asserts an element of inherent indeterminacy in economic relationships dependent upon human behavior. See J. Johnston, *Econometric Methods* (New York: McGraw Hill Book Company, Inc., 1960), pp. 5–7. Johnston notes that a distinction between the two rationalizations is not always practical but that the one based on omitted variables is essential while the second may be added.
2. See Johnston, p. 6, or N. R. Draper and H. Smith, *Applied Regression Analysis* (New York: John Wiley and Sons, 1966), p. 17.
3. See Arthur S. Goldberger, *Econometric Theory* (New York: John Wiley and Sons, Inc., 1964), pp. 238–239.

Chapter 3

1. Market Research Department of Fortune, *Fortune Plant and Product Directory: Of the 1000 Largest U.S. Industrial Corporations* (II Vols.; Time, Inc., 1966).

Chapter 4

1. See, for example, Carl Kaysen and D. F. Turner, *Antitrust Policy: An Economic and Legal Analysis* (Cambridge: Harvard University Press, 1959), p. 295.
2. Maxwell R. Conklin and Harold T. Goldstein, "Census Principles of Industry and Product Classification, Manufacturing Industries," in *Business Concentration and Price Policy* (Princeton: Princeton University Press, 1955), p. 5.
3. In particular, see the data from U.S. Department of Commerce Bureau of the Census, *1963 Census of Manufacturers, Vol. II: Industry Statistics, Part I: Major Groups 20–28* (Washington D.C.: U.S. Government Printing Office,

Chapter 5

1. See, for example, Kamerschen, pp. 432, 437; Bain, *Industrial Organization,* pp. 386–396; and Stigler, *Capital and Rates . . .* , pp. 51, 123–125.
2. *Moody's Industrial Manual* (New York: Moody's Investor Service Ltd., 1959). Also see volumes for 1960–1968.
3. Bain, *Industrial Organization,* p. 227. Comanor and Wilson, p. 234, argue further that to some extent, advertising expenditures may also be taken as a symptom of differentiation.
4. Joe S. Bain, *Barriers to New Competition* (Cambridge: Harvard University Press, 1962), pp. 123–124.
5. Bureau of Advertising of American Newspaper Publishers Association, *Expenditures of National Advertisers in Newspapers Year–1967* (New York, 1967), also for *Year–1960* and *Year–1956*; Institute of Outdoor Advertising, Inc., *Outdoor Advertising Expenditures* (Norwalk, Connecticut, 1967); Leading National Advertisers, Inc., *National Advertising Investments* (Norwalk, Connecticut, 1967), also for 1960 and 1956; Radio Expenditure Reports, *Radio: Network and Spot Radio Advertisers: Estimated Expenditures– National and Regional Advertisers* (Larchmont, New York, Quarterly, 1967); Television Bureau of Advertising, Inc., *Tenth Annual Spot Television Expenditure Report* (New York, 1965), also the *Fifth Annual, 1960* and *First Annual Report, 1956.*
6. See National Science Foundation, *Funds for Research and Development in Industry*, 1959 (Washington, D.C., 1962).
7. Annual data on patents secured by company are available in U.S. Patent Office, *Index of Patents Issued from the United States Patent Office 1959* (Washington, D.C., Government Printing Office, 1960), also for the years 1960–1968.
8. Federal Trade Commission, p. 10.
9. Franco Modigliani, "New Developments on the Oligopoly Front," *Journal of Political Economy,* 66 (June 1958), pp. 215–232.
10. Estimates of minimum efficient size plants are taken from the work of the National Commission on Food Marketing with the following exceptions: cigars, cigarettes, distilled liquors, and malt liquors. Estimates for these latter industries are based on survey data while the Commission's estimates are based on analyzing Census data using the survivor technique. Estimates are available for Census four-digit industries only. See National Commission on Food Marketing, *The Structure of Food Manufacturing,* Tech. Study No. 8 (Washington, D.C.: Government Printing Office, 1966), pp. 97–98.
11. W. J. Baumol, *Business Behavior, Value and Growth* (New York: John Wiley and Sons, Inc., 1968), p. 33.
12. See Hall and Weiss, p. 332 or FTC study, pp. 15–16.

13. For examples of structural arguments see Bain, *Industrial Organization*, p. 310; Richard Caves, *American Industry: Structure, Conduct, Performance*, 2nd ed. (Englewood Cliffs: Prentice Hall, Inc., 1967), pp. 30–31; or Kaysen and Turner, p. 105. References to growth as a part of basic economic data include Hall and Weiss, p. 323; and Kamerschen, pp. 436–437.
14. Stigler, *Capital and Rates of Return . . .* , p. 64.
15. Norman R. Collins and Lee E. Preston, "Concentration and Price Cost Margins in Food Manufacturing Industries," *Journal of Industrial Economics*, 14 (July 1966), p. 235.
16. Corwin D. Edwards, "Conglomerate Bigness as a Source of Power," *Business Concentration and Price Policy* (Princeton: Princeton University Press, 1955), pp. 331–352.
17. See for instance Donald Turner, "Conglomerate Mergers and Section 7 of the Clayton Act," *Harvard Law Review*, 78 (May 1965), pp. 1313–1365.
18. Comanor and Wilson, pp. 434–436.
19. Miller, p. 264.
20. Federal Trade Commission, p. 34.

Chapter 6

1. See Robert M. Solow, "Technical Change and the Aggregate Production Function," *Review of Economics and Statistics*, 39 (August 1957), pp. 312–320.
2. See Paul M. Hohenberg, *Chemicals in Western Europe: 1850–1914* (Chicago: Rand McNally, 1967).
3. F. M. Scherer, "Firm Size and Patented Inventions," *The American Economic Review*, 55 (December 1965), pp. 1097–1125.
4. Jesse W. Markham, "Market Structure, Business Conduct, and Innovation," *American Economic Review*, 55 (May 1965), p. 325.
5. See Joseph A. Schumpeter, *Capitalism, Socialism, and Democracy*, 3rd ed. (New York: Harper and Brothers, 1942), p. 82.
6. Schumpeter, p. 102.
7. For an excellent review, see F. M. Scherer, *Industrial Market Structure and Economic Performance* (Chicago: Rand McNally and Company, 1970), pp. 346–378.
8. See Richard R. Nelson, "The Simple Economics of Basic Scientific Research," *Journal of Political Economy*, 67 (June 1959), p. 303.
9. For data source, see U.S. Patent Office as previously cited.
10. Scherer, *Industrial Market . . .* , p. 361.

Chapter 7

1. Comanor and Wilson, p. 435.
2. Federal Trade Commission, p. 5.

3. See Johnston, pp. 148–150. The fact that we did not include a random measurement error in the dependent variable has no effect on the final conclusion.

Chapter 8

1. George J. Stigler, *The Organization of Industry* (Homewood, Illinois: Richard D. Irwin, Inc., 1968), p. 145.

Index

a priori reasoning, basis of, 83
absolute size, 72
acquisition, patterns of, 38
advertising, 46–47; expenditures, 14, 40–41; ratio, 53, 86–87; over sales, 41n, 48; variables, 47, 62, 69
after-tax profits, 86
aggregation: approaches, 12, 14; effects of, 13, 81–85; of firms, 29, 80; levels of, 1, 3, 77, 81–82
agencies, state, 1
agriculture, orientation, 2
antitrust laws, 10
assets, 21, 59
atomistic industries, 15
attitudes, entrepreneurial, 67
autocorrelation, 15, 69n; degree of, 85; disturbance terms, 17; market-related, 69; pattern of, 3; problem of, 88

Bain, Joe S., cited, 40, 59
baked goods, soft, 39
bankruptcy, pain of, 5
barriers: entry, 2, 7; plant scale, 44, 57, 87; selling costs to, 42n
Baumol, W. J., hypothesis of, 53, 57
behavior, competitive and noncompetitive, 6–8, 10
bigness, subject of conglomerate, 45, 67
binary variables, 60, 62, 67–70, 74
buy at par, 5

capital: equity, 47; market, 44; physical, 65; rates of return, 62n
census, 1, 44; data, 13, 39, 77, 79; definitions, 11, 40, 46–47, 69, 72–73; five-digit industries, 71; four-digit industries, 71, 75, 87–88; groupings, 2, 34; industries, 11, 35, 39–40, 46, 52, 54, 56–58, 62, 64, 69, 71, 86–88; three-digit system, 81; value, 78
Census, Bureau of the, 33–34
centralization, degree of, 6
chemicals, sectors as, 65, 67
class differences, pattern of, 47, 63
coefficients: estimated, 47, 57, 86; of multiple determination, 48, 51, 54; population, 84; regression, 48, 51, 54, 56, 70, 74
Collins, Norman R., cited, 13, 45
Comanor, William S., cited, 57, 62n, 81
Company: concentration ratio, 48, 51, 84; data, 12, 14; diversified, 22–23, 46, 66, 68, 85, 87; individual, 82–83; integrated, 38; management, 65; market power, 66; and monopoly, 86; profits, 15, 61, 64, 79, 87; sample, 30–31; specialized, 77–79, 81–83, 85; variables, 14, 77, 79
competition: degrees of, 6–7, 10, 86; levels of, 5, 10; meaning of, 10; minimum, 31; perfect, 5, 8–9; rigors of, 10, 57, 66, 86; stifling of, 66
common-market, related components, 80
concentration: absolute, 58; cumulative, 57–58; effects of, 57–58; evidence of, 86; information on, 11; levels of, 59; ratio, 57–63, 70, 74, 83, 86; and profits, 64, 82; relationship, 2, 13, 32, 72, 81; weighted, 60, 63; ratios, 57–61
conglomeration, operations, 15–16
constrained variables, 64
consumer: binary, 47; orientation, 69, 72; welfare, 8, 10
corn products, 67
corporation reports, 15, 39
costs, 10, 14, 66, 83
covariance matrix and terms, 3, 19, 22, 26
curvilinear forms, 59, 62

dairy products, fresh, 38–39
data: analysis of, 37, 79; availability of, 29, 32; basic economic, 7–8, 65
decision making, 6, 9
demand growth, measures of, 45
dependent variables, 12, 14, 37
depreciation, computation of, 38
differentiation, product, 7, 14, 17, 46–47, 57, 70, 72, 74, 86–87
discount, 5
disturbance term, error and variance of, 3, 82
diversification, problems of, 12, 15, 20–23, 26, 46, 62, 66, 68, 85, 87
duopolists, goals of, 7–8

econometric models, 5, 15, 17, 67–68, 87
Economic Research Service, 32
economy, the, 31, 44; data on, 7–8, 65; criteria for, 11, 33, 87; growth of, 65; and sales profit, 10, 17, 24, 29, 77, 83; review of, 34, 41n; theory on, 33
education, levels of, 87
Edwards, Corwin D., cited, 16, 45
electronics, 67
employment, 32, 38–39
environment, elements of, 6–7
entrepreneurs, attitudes of, 6, 67

113

equations, regression, 3, 54, 56, 70, 85; error terms of, 78, 80-81
equity, 21, 37-38, 47, 59
error: components, 23, 77; margins of, 63, 82, 85; measurements in, 83-84; terms, 3, 11, 17-26, 46, 68-69, 78, 80-81
estimates, procedures of, 3, 26, 29, 37, 47, 51, 64, 77, 81, 84-85, 87
expenditures: levels of, 12, 41, 47; market, 46-47; research and development, 48, 51, 54, 67, 87

Federal Trade Commission, 1, 3, 15, 39-40, 43-44, 58, 62n, 82, 87
field surveys, 31, 39
food sector, 1-2, 10, 14, 34, 37, 40, 48-51, 54-56, 67-70, 73-74, 87
foreign markets, 38
Fortune Plant and Product Directory, 29
France, progressiveness in, 65

Galbraith, John K., cited, 10
geography, influence of, 29, 38-39
Germany, progressiveness in, 65
goods and services, 38, 65
governmental controls, 1
Great Britain, progressiveness in, 65
Grether, E. T., cited, 15
gross national product, 65
group studies and procedures, 11, 13

Hall, Marshall, cited, 3, 44
Herfindahl index measures, 22-23, 68
heteroskedasticity, pattern of, 3, 15, 17, 26, 53, 68-69, 77-81, 85, 88
Hohenberg, Paul M., cited, 65

income, real, 33
identity matrix, 20, 26
independent variables, 12-18, 21, 38, 46, 53, 81, 84
industrial organization, 1-2, 11, 15, 37
industry: analysis, 78-79; definitions, 1, 5, 32-34, 39-40, 47, 53, 86-89; observations of, 77, 83; performance of, 6-7, 14-15, 31; structure of, 8, 39-40, 46
innovation, benefits from, 66, 72
input prices, 7
IQ research, 6
Internal Revenue Service (IRS), 12-13, 81
interviews, personal, 3
inventions, unanticipated, 66

Justice, Department of, 1

Kamerschen, David R., cited, 8, 15

least squares, 2, 83; classical (CLS), 3, 11, 15, 19-20, 26-27, 46-47, 51-54, 57, 62-64, 68-70, 74, 84, 88; generalized (GLS), 3, 17, 26, 46, 51, 53-54, 56-57, 70, 72, 74-75, 85-86, 88

management, quality of, 15, 17, 23, 43, 68, 85
marginal utilities, 8, 10
market, 25, 32; concentration, 60; defined, 5, 31, 83; foreign, 38; growth, 2, 45, 80; imperfections in, 44; observations, 78, 82; oligopolistic, 7; performance, 1-2, 7, 10, 17, 57, 65; power, 72; related variables, 14, 17-18, 21-22, 24, 47, 78, 81, 83-84; sector studies, 13-14, 81; single, 17, 84; structures, 1, 6-9, 12, 65, 87
Markham, Jesse W., cited, 65
Mason, Edward S., cited, 6
maximization, 6, 9
McGraw-Hill Book Company, 32, 39n
measurements, 86-87
microeconomic theory, 6, 83
Miller, Richard A., cited, 58, 86
Modigliani, Franco, cited, 44
monopoly: consequences of, 8-9; curbing of, 1; power of, 10, 66, 69, 86; and profits, 10; pure, 6-7
Moody's Industrial Manual, 38
multimarket boundaries, 16, 57, 61, 79, 82, 84

national brands, 14
National Science Foundation, 41
natural resources, conservation of, 7
Nelson, Richard R., hypothesis of, 66-67, 72, 87
neo-Schumpeterian hypotheses, 11, 66-67, 87
new products, growth of, 10-11, 65
nonfood operations, 29, 68-74, 87
nonlinear forms, 59-62

oligopoly, theory of, 7, 66
omega matrix, 19-22, 27, 69, 75, 78
omega ratio, 19, 46, 56-57, 69-72, 86, 88
opportunity, scientific, 65; technological, 69n
output, level of, 5, 9; per worker, 65

par, buying at, 5
parameters, estimates of, 3, 18, 26
patents, number issued, 67, 73
performance: dimensions of, 9, 65; market, 7; structure scheme of, 2, 5, 11
personal interviews, 3

population, influence of, 3, 17, 60, 79, 81
Preston, Lee F., cited, 13, 45
price: level changes, 38; premiums, 5; theory, 5-10, 15, 85
private labels, 14, 31, 43
procurement, structure of, 2, 69
product differentiation, 2, 7, 14, 17, 29, 40-43, 46-47, 57, 70, 72, 74, 86-87; sales, 1, 31; transformation function, 8
production, cost of, 6-7, 9, 65
profit: after-tax, 86; analysis of, 77, 82; constraints on, 6; determination, 10, 15, 86; long-run, 5; net, 47; policy on, 6, 29, 60-61; rate of, 2-3, 8, 10-15, 20, 38, 53, 57-59, 79-80, 83, 85, 87; ratio of to sales, 10-11, 17, 24; relationship of, 27, 64, 68, 81-82; total, 37-38
progressiveness, industrial, 1, 3, 7-11, 65, 68, 88
promotional programs, 7

quantitative research, survey of, 11
Quarterly Journal of Economics, 42n
questionnaires, 3

radio, 41
rate of return, 2, 13-14, 47, 60, 62n, 64, 68-79, 82-83, 86
raw materials, availability of, 65
regression, multiple, 2-3, 21, 37, 54, 56, 62-63, 70, 85
research: empirical, 7, 10, 67; industrial, 11; I.Q., 6; investment in, 69; methodology and programs of, 1, 3, 14, 27, 29, 37, 66, 88
Research and Development (R & D), 1, 8, 41-42, 46-48, 51, 53-54, 67, 86-87
residuals, examination and patterns of, 60, 68-69, 87; squared, 52-53
resources, allocation of, 14
retailing distribution system, 2
revenue, marginal, 6

sales: breakdowns of, 32; foreign, 38; percentage, 14, 21, 67; and profit from, 59; sector, 80-81
Scherer, F. M., cited, 8, 65, 69n, 72, 87
Schumpeter, Joseph A., cited, 10-11, 65-66; hypothesis of, 67, 87
sector observation and sales, 80-81
sellers and selling industry, competitiveness of, 6-7, 10, 33
sensitivity analysis, spirit of, 2, 46-47, 53, 85, 88
single-product enterprises, 20, 26
squared residuals, table on, 52-53
Solow, Robert M., 65
storage, costs of, 5
Standard-Industrial Classification (SIC), 12-13, 29, 33, 81
statistics, tests of significance, 18, 86, 88
step-functional relationships, 60-61
Stigler, George J., cited, 13, 45, 62n 86
structure-progress relationships, 10-11, 15, 27, 37, 67, 69n, 88
substitutes, use of, 5
sugar-refining industry, 34
surveys, accuracy of, 31-32, 39

taxes, 38, 86
technology, changes in, 7, 34, 65-67, 72, 87
telephone, interviews over, 3
television, 41
trade publications, 39
transformation function, 9
transportation, 5

United States Department of Agriculture, (USDA), 39a
utilities, marginal, 8

variance-covariance matrix, 26

Weiss, Leonard W., cited, 3, 41n, 44
wholesaling distribution system, 2
Williamson, Oliver E., cited, 42n
Wilson, Thomas A., 57, 62n, 81

About the Authors

Blake Imel is an Agricultural Economist in the Competition and Pricing Branch of the Marketing Economics Division of the U.S. Department of Agriculture, where he has worked since 1968. He received his B.S. in agricultural economics from Purdue University in 1966, and his Ph.D. in the same field from the University of Wisconsin, Madison in 1971.

Michael Behr is Director of the Center for Economic Education and Associate Professor of Business and Economics at the University of Wisconsin, Superior. He studied agricultural economics at the University of Minnesota, where he received his B.S. and M.S. and was an instructor of economics, and at the University of Wisconsin, Madison, where he received his Ph.D. in 1969.

Peter Helmberger is a professor in the Department of Agricultural Economics at the University of Wisconsin, Madison. He received his B.S. in economics and M.S. in agricultural economics from the University of Minnesota, and his Ph.D. in agricultural economics from the University of California in 1961, and has taught at universities since then. He is co-author of *Cooperative Bargaining in Agriculture: Grower-Processor Markets for Fruits and Vegetables* (1965) and has written numerous chapters in books and articles in professional journals.